Truth &
Democracy

To those who desire greater truth

in their democracies and lives

Truth & Democracy

*Truth as a Guide for
Personal and Political Action
in an Age of Polarization*

by

Steve Zolno

REGENT PRESS
Berkeley, California

paperback:
ISBN 13: 978-1-58790-499-8
ISBN 10: 1-58790-499-3

e-book:
ISBN 13: 978-1-58790-525-4
ISBN: 10: 1-58790-525-6

Library of Congress Cataloging-in-Publication Data

Names: Zolno, Steve, author.
Title: Truth & democracy : truth as a guide for personal and political action in an age of polarization / Steve Zolno.
Other titles: Truth and democracy
Description: Berkeley, California : Regent Press, [2020] | Includes bibliographical references. | Summary: "Democracy is in crisis in the United States and in many countries around the world. Democracies are forged in the wake of oppression. At first there is trust among those with a common cause. But maintaining unity is a continual challenge. Many nations that started on a path to democracy in this century now are reverting to autocracy. Their elected leaders maintain support by pitting one part of the population against the other as they threaten those who challenge them. They exert their authority by repeating mistruths and intimidating the press. Internal divisions in the United States now threaten that it will tread that path. In the US and other democracies equality and human dignity still have not fully been realized. In every generation we must renew our commitment to democratic principles and their meaning for our time"-- Provided by publisher.
Identifiers: LCCN 2020020881 (print) | LCCN 2020020882 (ebook) | ISBN 9781587904998 (trade paperback) | ISBN 9781587905254 (kindle edition)
Subjects: LCSH: Democracy--Philosophy. | Truth--Political aspects. | Political ethics. | Political participation. | Political culture.
Classification: LCC JC423 .Z66 2020 (print) | LCC JC423 (ebook) | DDC
    321.8--dc23
LC record available at https://lccn.loc.gov/2020020881
LC ebook record available at https://lccn.loc.gov/2020020882

Regent Press
Berkeley, California
www.regentpress.net
regentpress@mindspring.com

Contents

Acknowledgements

In June, 2018, a group of 21 friends provided me with feedback on the first draft of this book. The message was kind but clear: the points in the book need to be backed by more cogent arguments.

I have worked on living up to that counsel since that time, but have found that describing the nature of truth, and especially its relationship to democracy, to be a challenge. Hopefully the effort before you fulfills the faith of those who have spent much time and energy providing me their perspective.

I am indebted to the following for their input on making this book the most effective work on truth – and its implications for democracy – that I could create: Jake Birnburg, Wyndy Knox Carr, Hannah Cohen, Carol Delton, Brooks Dyer, Len Fellman, Lawrence Fleury, Bob Forman, Jeanne Forman, Chia Hamilton, Dennis Kaplan, Rob Katz, Alex Madonik, Will Ozier, Cathy Sillavo, Dan Shiner, Eve Sweetser, Emily Toch, Herb Tate, Mary Warner, and Mark Weiman.

The book's shortcomings of course are the responsibility of its author.

Introduction –
Why this book?

Democracy is in crisis in the United States and in many countries around the world.

Democracies are forged in the wake of oppression. At first there is trust among those with a common cause, but maintaining unity is a continual challenge. In ancient Athens, the establishment of democracy – Greek for "government by the people" – inspired a sense of shared purpose, but then Athens was wrought by internal divisions.[1] The English struggled between monarchy and rebellion from the time of the Magna Carta. The founders of the American republic feuded over how democracy should be run. Leaders of the French Revolution engaged in an orgy of violence against each other.

Many nations that started on a path to democracy in this century – Russia, Poland, India, Venezuela and the Philippines to name a few – now are reverting to autocracy. Their elected leaders maintain support by pitting one part of the population against the other as they threaten those who challenge them. They exert their authority by repeating mistruths and intimidating the press.[2]

Internal divisions in the United States now threaten that it will tread that path. The Declaration of Independence – launched during the American Revolution – established human equality as the most essential truth of democracy. But for over 200 years there has been a struggle between those with different views about how to make democracy a lived reality. Those who want life, liberty, and the pursuit of happiness for themselves are not always keen on ensuring these benefits for others.

Perhaps what most impels people to rebel is a lack of recognition – a feeling that they are not considered valid human beings. In autocracies major decisions are made for people. Their right to think for themselves, to come to their own truths, and to act on those truths is denied. But in places where rebellion overthrows the yoke of tyranny, people often seek a return to an authority figure to provide certainty in an uncertain world.

Since the inception of democracy there have been those who want to be active participants, and those who prefer to delegate decisions to others on the assumption that all will work out. But simply trusting our leaders often results in disappointment. We may be clear that we don't want oppression, but rarely focus on clarifying what we do want.

If the truth is that all are created equal then everyone is entitled to being treated with respect. If we want to live in a society that promotes human dignity then we need to support leaders who are champions of that view. To avoid a return to autocracy we each must take active responsibility for maintaining our freedom and that of others. When we delegate this to politicians or political parties – and fail to monitor them – we take ourselves out of the decision-making process. When we let leaders do our thinking for us we no longer are free.

In the United States, "We the People" are the authority for the nation's Constitution and laws. But the US founders created an imperfect union with a great amount of inequality, including discrimination toward women and harsh treatment of minorities.

The government that represents us must act based on what seems true at any point in time. When we find that our old truths no longer serve us, then they – and our actions based on them – must change to fit the new reality. Human rights and equality have evolved, but still remain largely unfulfilled. Many people still do not experience the benefits of an equal society in employment, housing, and the administration of justice.

In democracies, our representatives act in our name. Thus we must be clear in our own minds about democratic values and how they apply in the real world. We then can work together toward that which best serves the whole. When we abdicate our responsibility any type of abuse can be done in our name – to others and even to ourselves.

In our day, people are choosing sides and increasingly unwilling to consider the view of anyone who sees the world through a different lens. When intolerance dominates in a democracy it moves us back in the direction of the autocracy it once overcame.

How did we get to this point? Is there a truth beyond our partisan views and if such a truth exists how do we find it and bring it into our democracies and lives?

We always have a choice about whether to pursue inclusive truths that best serve us all, or to be swayed by those who preach exclusive truths that divide us.[3]In all of our interactions we choose between the democratic value of universal respect and the autocratic value of discord.

In the US – and other democracies – the meaning of words like equality and human dignity only slowly have become apparent and still have not fully been realized. In every generation we must renew our commitment to democratic principles and their meaning for our time. What follows is my hopeful contribution toward that effort.

Why Truth is Essential for a Viable Democracy

KEY PRINCIPLE: *The success of democracy depends on a commitment to the pursuit of truth by both societies and individuals.*

In democracies, "We the People"[4] decide which politicians and policies to support. We expect our leaders to maintain prosperity and keep our country secure. But those who would lead us present drastically different views about the best path forward, so how do we know who to support? How can we determine which ideas and actions are most likely to maintain democracy and the freedoms it is designed to protect?

Democracy was born when people who believed that they were treated unfairly reclaimed their dignity and rights. They resented having their interests overlooked and insisted on recognition as valid human beings. But those who assume power – even with broad support – often ignore or forget the past. Democracy is threatened when leaders refuse to extend equal rights and dignity to those they govern or when the truth they promote is that the interests of part of the population are more important than those of others.

To make democracy work we must put leaders in place who understand its principles and how best to implement them. But that requires voters who also understand those principles. This book is about how to identify the most important ideas that underlie democracy and how to put them into practice.

The essential truth upon which democracy is based is that all individuals are equally valid human beings, deserving of dignity and respect. In a well-functioning democracy the interests of all are considered equally important and taken into account, or in the words of Lincoln, democracy is "Dedicated to the proposition that all (persons) are created equal."[5] This is what separates democracies from governments ruled by and for only some of the people.

When democracies work as intended, leaders create and enforce laws equally. They set a moral tone and models for our actions – they are teachers as well as law-makers. In democracies it is the role of leaders to address the needs of those in all walks of life. This is best done based on input from the brightest minds available who are attuned to democratic values. But the ultimate authority always is the voice of the people expressed via elections.

Nations move farther from democracy when leaders are more concerned with promoting their personal interests than those of the people they serve – when they use falsehoods designed to pit people against each other to increase their personal power. This is why honest and open communication about how best to meet the needs of people is essential to make democracies work.

Facts are not the same as truth. Facts are verifiable events upon which all can agree. We come to our ideas about truth based on our interpretation of facts. We may see the sun rise and fall daily and reasonably conclude that it revolves around the earth. Our concepts usually become more accurate – both as individuals and a society – after continued observation and reflection. But when we cling to our concepts regardless of the truths that are revealed by further inquiry, they fail to align with reality. The best leaders acknowledge the truths dictated by facts. They learn from and base their actions on those truths; they don't ignore them or try to manipulate them for their own purposes.

When we are open to new truths – tempered by the interpretation of facts after long-term observation – our concepts often will be forced to change.We see the sun rising and setting, but because of what we have learned over time we no longer believe that it revolves around the earth. We might make assumptions about people based on race or religion, but with more interaction and observation we may move beyond our stereotypes. In a court of law, where the jury system is an essential element of democracy, we may or may not vote for conviction after careful consideration of all the evidence. In the realm of politics, our entrenched views might budge a bit with exposure to a variety of perspectives.

So how is it that people see the same facts and come to different conclusions? Each of us are individuals with different backgrounds and beliefs developed over time. Our actions are based on ideas we hold about what is true or right. We process new information through the beliefs we already hold, which can become entrenched.[6] We often build walls around our views to support what we believe, and keep out what we don't want to hear. We may support individuals or political parties that align with our views without considering whether they are advancing the democratic principle of human equality.

With the divisive points of view in our society, is it even possible for us to arrive at an understanding of what ideas and actions benefit everyone? Since there are many views about how democracy best functions, how do we know which ideas to support?

The limits to what we know

Although we may seek truth to guide our actions, our information always will be limited in all areas including science, politics, and even what we know about each other. But we still need to act, and we base our actions on the knowledge we have. If we hope to come closer to an understanding of what is true we must open ourselves to considering that there may be other valid viewpoints than those we hold. When we stick with our concepts regardless of the evidence, we become out of touch with reality. This can result in actions that have negative effects on our lives and those around us. If our navigation system is based on false information we will constantly be running into walls. Although we must act on the truths we have, our view from tomorrow may be very different from what it is today.

Repeated observations – by individuals over their lifetimes and societies over centuries – have brought us closer to aligning our ideas with what is true, and we have acted on those truths to advance our civilizations. For the time that there been *Homo sapiens* on earth – perhaps 200,000 years – our progress has been incremental but enormous. We have come to understand much of the nature of the universe and have used that knowledge to make our lives more secure.

During our earliest time on earth we belonged to small tribes where individuals worked together for the benefit of the group.[7] As our social units expanded from tribe to city to state, major decisions were made by leaders who were at a greater distance from those they governed. Societies became divided into rulers and those who were ruled, with the assumption that the judgments of those in positions of power are superior. This can be seen in the development of the civilization of Egypt over a period of 3,000 years.[8]

Large civilizations go back at least 6,000 years, beginning with Mesopotamia (what is now Iraq).[9] Those in power had the final word on what would be regarded as just and true. Any deviation from their laws was considered a challenge to authority that would lead to a deterioration of society. Their Code of Ur-Nammu, found on clay tablets from about 2000 BCE, is the oldest known written law. It mentions equality and truth, but mainly describes punishments for infractions.

To impose uniform thought and action, rulers taught that their truths were infallible and supported by the gods. They maintained that their tribe or nation was superior to others, which helped keep subjects loyal, but this also contributed to rivalry and war. An example was the war between Athens and Sparta in the 5th century BCE. And as we can see, the tradition of tribalism – devotion to one's own group over others – continues into our own day.

People in societies throughout the world were divided into those who ruled and those who lived in subjugation for most of history. Ancient Chinese emperors burned books – along with their authors – to keep them from exploring independent truths.[10] The leaders of the Inquisition also burned the books and bodies of those who dared challenge their truths, including the idea that the earth is the center of the universe.[11]

The Origins of Democracy

Hierarchical society was challenged by the introduction of democracy in Athens. Farmers composed a large segment of the population that needed to borrow in poor harvests. They sank steadily into greater debt and servitude. That system was upended by their leader Solon, who in about 600 BCE was concerned about the deterioration of Athenian society due to extreme inequality.[12] He reversed the debt of the large rural class while affirming its humanity. This led to democracy in Athens and set an example for Western democracies centuries later.

The word democracy is a Greek term that means "government by the people." The Athenians extended citizenship to males from a broad economic spectrum which was a radical idea for the time. Their guiding truth – as stated by their leader Pericles in his famous Funeral Oration – was that all men deserve equal treatment and opportunity.

Our constitution…favors the many instead of the few; this is why [our state] is called a democracy. If we look to the laws, they afford equal justice to all in their private differences; if no social standing, advancement in public life falls to reputation for capacity, class considerations not being allowed to interfere with merit; nor again does poverty bar the way, if a man is able to serve the state, he is not hindered by the obscurity of his condition.[13]

The most essential truths about democracy in our day are contained in the 1776 **Declaration of Independence** of the United States, the founding document of the world's first modern democracy.

We hold these truths to be self-evident, that all men are created equal, that they are endowed by their creator with certain unalienable rights, that among these are life, liberty and the pursuit of happiness.

At its founding the US fell very short of implementing the principle of equality. Inequality was an integral part of a country that featured slavery, war against Native Americans, and second-class citizenship for women.

In our time we have gone far beyond the US founders in our understanding of how to implement equality. The Fourteenth Amendment to the Constitution, written after the Civil War, guarantees "equal protection of the laws." Most democracies have moved closer to the fulfillment of this concept in their laws and personal interactions. They have more fully – but not totally – included women and minorities as equals in areas such as voting and employment. But within democracies there still are those who resist the extension of human rights to those they consider less than equal to themselves.

In our systems of government – as well as our

interactions with others – we use one of two truths as our guide: (1) all human beings are equally important and deserve equal rights and opportunities, or (2) some people are less important than others and do not deserve equal treatment. Only laws and practices that support equality are compatible with democracy.

Democracy is government by and for the people – all the people. Government by and for a few – or even a majority – no longer is democracy. Organizations, families, and schools, as well as governments, can be democratic. In these situations the needs and viewpoints of all are taken into account. When a society is too large for direct democracy, it is the role of representatives to act in the best interest of all their constituents.

Autocracies or oligarchies – run by one person or a small group – by their nature deny the "self-evident truth" that all are created equal. In these situations the welfare and opinions of large parts of the population are ignored. People are judged by their political status, wealth, or the groups to which they belong rather than their value as individuals.

Human equality always was – and still is – a radical concept. Although easy to state, its implementation is difficult. The challenge is determining what it looks like in the real world. Just like ancient Athens, the early American republic made a great leap forward in recognizing the value of every human being, but fell far short of fully implementing that idea. Even in countries that consider themselves democratic, privilege and wealth still confer an advantage.

The US founders studied history going back to ancient times. They got many of their ideas from the

Enlightenment writers of their day, including Locke, Rousseau, and Voltaire. They taught that human equality is a basic truth and that an unjust government should be overturned when it violates human dignity. But is the implementation of the idea of human equality really possible, or only a fantasy that never will come to pass? Is equality a truth that can guide us, or just an ideal that cannot really be fulfilled? To explore these questions we need to consider the nature of truth itself.

The Nature of Truth

We all are truth seekers. But our society's idea of what is true changes over time. All we once needed were local truths. Our skills included how best to hunt or gather food, and then as we became agricultural societies, new understanding provided success at raising our crops and animals. Slow progress since then has led to the technological society we have today.

Humans are unique in their ability to revise their models of what is true – both as individuals and across generations. At birth we don't differentiate between objects or make judgments about what is good or bad. We enthusiastically observe and explore our surroundings. We slowly form concepts based on interaction with our environment and guidance from others, including parents, relatives, teachers, and friends.[14]

Our ideas about the world – and the words we use to describe it – begin to substitute for observation at an early age. As we learn names for objects and people we become less aware of their uniqueness. The person with the smiling face and gentle voice that feels good close up becomes "mom," and that other person with the deeper voice becomes "dad." The object with a seat, four legs and a back becomes a "chair," and that other object with a top and four legs becomes a "table." [15]

We also learn words to describe actions like eating, talking and walking. Our concepts allow us to function more effectively, but as we do, we sacrifice the accuracy that comes from close attention to our surroundings. We replace observations with ideas that further shape our view of the world. Most chairs and tables are very different from others – as are people – but we force our labels on them as we ignore their uniqueness. We then make our observations fit the concepts already established in our minds.

As we continue our education we build on the truths we have come to believe. We are taught more abstract concepts like those contained in mathematics, science, or history. As we integrate these into our minds we begin to develop and convey our own ideas. But much of our education is repeating the "truths" of teachers or texts that may have little relevance to our observations. We are taught to accept what we are told rather than come to our own conclusions based on experience.

By the end of childhood we have developed our basic ideas about what is true regarding others, our world, and ourselves. But the concepts we have developed dictate where we look and what we see.[16] If we develop an affinity – or dislike – for some individuals or members of racial, religious, or ethnic groups, we will interpret their actions to confirm the positive or negative views we already hold. If we prefer certain foods or sports or styles, much of our attention will be focused on these areas to the exclusion of others. We continue to engage with people, the media, books and other sources to seek truth. But our concepts limit our view of reality. We force our world into preset categories and thereby miss much of its essence.

In any moment I only can focus on a small part of the world around me. What I see is based on the lens I carry within me. With these limits to my perception, is it even possible to know what is true?

The "truth" of my immediate world as I write this is a computer screen on a desk in front of me. But this only is a small part of what is in the room. A complete account could be endless. I am leaving out a plant on my desk, the soil and pot it sits in, and the fact that it is leaning toward the light. I have omitted the color of the desk and the speakers beside my screen. I've ignored a glass of water and its crystallized design, a photo of a sunset on the wall, a printer, posters, mirrors, the texture of the floor, and infinite possibilities for just this one room. For a preverbal six-month old everything would be of interest, but the nature of language forces me to choose what seems most significant to comprehend and describe my surroundings.

The setting in which you are reading this also contains much more than you can fully describe. But to communicate in our world of words we need to fit what we see into familiar terms and ignore most of what is around us. We focus only on what we think is needed for our comprehension and description.

We also reduce other people to our concepts. We see more detail of those we know or who we think are like us, and put those who are unfamiliar into

23

pre-set categories. This blinds us to much of the truth of others. The bias of those who consider themselves members of one group toward others is common and well-documented.[17]

We often get our ideas of what is true or right from those we admire or those who act confidently – parents, celebrities, historical figures, religious models. We shape our beliefs and model our behavior on them. Ideas expressed emotionally by others affect our own emotions.

Now let's discuss you for a moment. Your name is the label used to identify you, but it doesn't begin to describe who you are. You have innumerable characteristics that include your appearance, your talents, your aspirations, your fears, your ever-changing thoughts and feelings, your observations, your likes and dislikes, your relationships, your racial or religious identity, your strengths and weaknesses. These only are a few of the areas that would provide a deeper understanding if we were to more fully describe you. As we label people we ignore that their true nature is complex. Much of who we are remains unknown, which is why many people consider themselves misunderstood.

The views we adopt determine the world we see and affect our relationships with others. Each of us is right from our own point of view. If we have come to assume that others are supportive of us, we will see the obstacles we encounter as temporary. But if our truth becomes that others are against us, our path will seem blocked. We may bring optimism – or pessimism – to our interactions with the world, which will affect our satisfaction and success. We also may find ourselves moving back and forth between the two. We may come to believe that some people are good or bad – to be trusted or not – based solely on appearance or background. Our views become part of our identity; we consider any challenge of them to be a threat.[18]

Our moods also can affect how we see others and the world. Sometimes we react spontaneously, and at other times we reflect and take a more long-term view. At times we are more subjective and at other times more objective, more irrational or rational, more reactive or contemplative. We also have a compassionate side and a judgmental side. The first brings us closer to people, and the second keeps us at a distance. Acting rationally is usually what works in our best interest, but sometimes situations require immediate action and we don't have the time to think before we act.[19]

We often blame people for our positive or negative frame of mind. Being aware of that allows us to see how we harm ourselves by putting a wall between ourselves and others. Moving beyond blame allows us to experience our shared humanity and realize that others are vulnerable beings like ourselves. We then may shift our view a bit to see the world from their perspective. And in the moment we recognize our connections we experience the recognition we seek.

If we want to live in a world where we are valued, we must move toward one where all are valued. If we want to live in a world where we are respected, we must work toward respect for every human being. These are the most democratic values. As we judge others we experience the judgment we fear, but in the moment we move past judgment of others we also do this for ourselves. The

25

truths we live by affect our own well-being. In this way we create the world in which we live.

Truth and Democracy

Human equality, the truth upon which democracy is founded, is more easily stated than implemented. The founders of both the Athenian and the US democracies created government models based on equality, but being human, often disagreed and maneuvered against each other, as do leaders right up to our own day. If we find ourselves mired in cynicism about democracy's future how do we turn that around to realign with its ideals? Some answers might be found by using truth itself as our guide.

Our original view of the world was one of wholeness. We then gradually divided it into segments based on our concepts. But reality is beyond our concepts. Truth is not partisan; it is not the view of any one person, political party or religion. Humans progress when their search for truth supersedes preconception and partisanship. We move toward greater understanding of our world and other people when we put our judgments aside in humble acknowledgement of the limits of our understanding. But this leaves us needing to admit that we really don't know the whole truth.

Most disciplines – science, math, history, etc. – have progressed by continually reexamining our world to arrive at models that more accurately fit reality. But our concepts (or equations or formulas) never are complete descriptions of what is true. We frame our world as best we can while the bulk of it is ignored. Our thoughts and descriptions exclude much more than they include, but most progress has been made where free inquiry is encouraged in pursuit of truth. This is why democracies have represented much of the world's progress in numerous areas over the last two hundred years.

Wherever tyranny is established – and it is prevalent in human history – those who are oppressed harbor a hope for freedom. People consider themselves oppressed when they are told what to do and believe. Human dignity always awaits an opportunity to emerge. But throughout history there also has been a gradual evolution toward greater equality and an increased emphasis on the value of human beings.

Where does this vision of equality come from? Since we are born without a sense of a separate self, no one comes out of the womb believing her or himself superior or inferior. As we learn who we think we are – male or female, members of a race, religion or other group, in possession of particular talents, having or lacking confidence or self-esteem – we begin to set ourselves apart from others. But that view – although helpful for individual identity and survival – also can lead to a sense of separateness and the idea that our well-being must be achieved at the expense of others.

Hierarchies are common among humans – and in the animal kingdom – despite our instinct for equality.[20] Some people are smarter in some ways, some have better leadership skills, some are more confident. Only in our species has survival been tied to expanding our membership from family to tribe to nation with the possibility of cooperation for the benefit of all. We have advanced when we have expanded our group identity to more of humanity and regressed when we created enmity with those we consider different from ourselves.

When we hold the view that we all are equally valuable we see our welfare tied to that of others. We understand that our well-being is connected to that of the entire human race and what we do to others and our planet is what we do to ourselves. This corresponds to the most basic teachings of our major religions and lessons from philosophy, sociology, psychology, and science that the welfare of everyone is intertwined. It also is the most essential view of the founders of democracies.

In the following chapters I have outlined ten areas in which the truth we hold – human equality or its opposite – positively or negatively affects each of us, others, and our planet. Many other areas could be considered, but these examples establish the principle that the truth by which we live profoundly affects our lives in the present and for the future. They make it clear that a commitment to the idea of human equality is essential to the survival of democracy and our planet.

The topics of the following chapters are:

1. Interpersonal Relationships
2. Politics
3. Education
4. Economics
5. Science
6. The Environment
7. Health
8. Religion
9. Justice
10. International Relations

Truth and Action

The nature of the universe is ongoing change. Within societies – and individuals – the idea of what is true also changes over time. Ultimate truth is – and will remain – beyond our ability to fully describe, so we must humbly seek to understand it as best we can.

Building on our observations has led to knowledge that enables our civilizations to exist. An array of discoveries has allowed us to move from raw encounter with our environment to relatively comfortable lifestyles for most, if not all.

The truths we hold are primarily of value to the extent that they guide our actions. Our models of the world are the truths by which we live, based on our own insights and of those who have seen farther than ourselves. They provide the basis of our plans for the future. But we often encounter situations that don't fit our models. The world of concepts in which we live is not the real one, but only the best we have at any one time. Our ideas often come up short due to the gap between our minds and reality.

Our models continue to evolve as old ones fall away. Experience and experimentation force new insights upon us. The discovery of the solar system by Galileo, gravity by Newton, and relativity by Einstein all flew in the face of the conventional knowledge of their time.

But we still need to determine our goals and the actions we will take to move toward them. We do this based on the limited information we have at any one time. The current scientific consensus – based on centuries of careful observation – is the reality most likely to serve our needs.

Our ideas become set, but the world continually surprises us. When circumstances fail to meet my expectations I can focus on my disappointment – on who or what to blame – or acknowledge the limitations of my model and continue to revise it. If we are to move forward as individuals and as a society, being right or wrong is less important than refocusing and realigning our views with an expanding understanding of our world.

Acknowledging our limits forces us to observe more carefully and listen to others more openly. It causes us to be more in touch with the reality around us rather than our inner echo of the past. As we do this we begin to be more fully in tune with others and our world. We see that no one person has a monopoly on truth. This is the great equalizer. Continually revising our ideas requires humility, but our reward is a greater grasp of truth and more effective action. We also see the importance of seeking input of others for our decisions. This is democracy in action.

We have been the most successful species on earth so far because of our ability to absorb information and build on our understanding. We have created our own environments – including shelters and ways to feed ourselves – as we have moved from the state of hunter-gatherer to a civilization supported by agriculture. We have accumulated and continue to pass on knowledge that has sustained us to create our world.

We are blind to the future, but the greatest threat to our progress is stagnation. If our knowledge fails to evolve to meet ongoing challenges we are in danger of joining numerous species and civilizations that were successful only to the point where they didn't adapt.

With the continual threats to our democracies and planet – brought on mainly by ourselves – we must work together with a new urgency. The greatest progress occurs where people are universally respected; where they are free to think and create viable solutions to the challenges of their day; where innovation is encouraged and the best minds work together to discover and apply new understanding. Because democracies are designed to work that way it is no coincidence that they are environments that most support progress that benefits the entire human race.

No one can give us a guide for how to act in every moment. My hope is to provide insight into determining for ourselves how best to act in alignment with the truth of human equality that is the basis of democracy. This is the best path forward for what is just and likely to enhance our survival.

Acknowledging human equality on a daily basis allows us to begin shedding the prejudices we have adopted – knowingly or unknowingly – and continue to move toward creating the world in which we want to live. This is the surest route for democracy's success.

1. Interpersonal Relations

KEY PRINCIPLE: *Relationships that reflect democracy are based on trust and the idea that every person is an equally valuable human being.*

From the time that Homo sapiens appeared on earth, about 200,000 years ago, we improved our chances at survival by joining tribes. As we developed agricultural settlements around 12,000 years ago we were expected to sublimate our aggression for the benefit of the whole, and this allowed us to expand our social units to cities and states. The human tendency for antisocial behavior was recognized by ancient rulers who established strict laws to keep their societies functioning.[21]

We were able to create civilizations because we became social beings. The advent of democracy reflected a belief that we no longer need to be ruled by others; that we can set aside our enmity to work together for the common good. But this is more easily said than done.

Democracy – and tyranny – exist not only in governments, but in the minds and lives of people. Democracies are conceived in trust that they will provide fair and equal treatment for all. But we also have an instinct for hierarchy that can lead to tyranny.[22]

When we believe that our rights are threatened, the result may be outrage or revolution. But after revolution we engage in conflict about how to make democracy work, with each faction believing its views superior to the others. Our greatest challenge is agreeing on a common vision and developing the trust to sustain it.

The democracy of Athens was built on trust among its citizens and faith that their representatives would do what was best for them and the state. Thucydides, who chronicled Greece during its Golden Age (around 450 BCE) wrote that Athens was a place of "mutual politeness and lack of spite between...citizens, for the deep respect for law it inculcated, and for drawing to the city the fruits and products of the whole world."[23]

The slow progress of England toward democracy began with the Magna Carta of 1215, which established a degree of trust between King John and his nobles. The establishment of the House of Commons in the last half of that century moved the English toward a greater level of trust in their government. But that trust didn't last. It was marred by violent struggles for hundreds of years until the monarchy was overthrown during the English Revolution and Civil Wars of the 1600s. The monarchy was replaced with more tyranny under The Commonwealth before it again was restored.

The revolution of thirteen American colonies that began in 1775 created trust and mutual resolve by people at all levels of society as they struggled to overcome what they saw as a common enemy. They built a government based on the principle of human equality. But soon they engaged in partisan bickering, including a long dispute between Jefferson and Adams, and the famous feud between Hamilton and Burr.

Since that time, democracy has been tried in over 100 countries. After throwing off tyranny, which provided a common cause, many efforts at democracy have floundered when people turned their distrust toward each other. These conflicts continue into our own time.

The 1789 French Revolution was founded on "liberty, equality and fraternity." But it soon regressed into violence among its leaders because of conflicting visions and a power struggle about how best to implement those principles.

And in this century, many countries that built democracies on trust as they overthrew tyranny – including Poland, Hungary, and Brazil – now are threatened by factional fighting. There even has been physical fights among lawmakers.[24]

People commonly band together with others they consider members of their group – those of their ethnicity, religion, politics, gender, world view or financial status – to advocate for their rights. But often they are less concerned about the rights of those outside their group. This form of "populism" can result in dominance of some people over others and attacks against those with whom they disagree or don't like. It has undermined equality in many countries, including pre-World War II Germany and Italy, postwar Russia and China, and other countries that have moved in an authoritarian direction in our day, such as Turkey and Venezuela.

Equal rights for "We the People" – all the people

– is the essential principle that enables democracy to succeed. This requires dialogue in our governments, organizations, and personal interactions to forge a common path based on trust. Only a commitment to resolve issues between those with different views can lead to democracy that works for all.

We each consider ourselves accurate observers of others and the world. We have spent years learning about the nature of people and believe that we basically understand them. We pride ourselves on having attained a considerable amount of wisdom that we want to share. We think of ourselves as basically good people with honorable intentions who at times are misunderstood.

But if we were to be totally honest we would find that the truth is somewhat different. If we observed ourselves carefully we might be forced to conclude that there is a considerable gap between how we think we interact and the reality. We compare people with our standards of how they should look and act. We judge others personally rather than just disagreeing. We divide people into those who we think are like us and those who are not. We often focus on our judgments rather than acknowledging others as the unique individuals that they are.[25]

Our tribal self still is very much alive. It prompts us to see the "other" as an enemy not quite as human as ourselves. It mandates that we divide people into "us" and "them," right and wrong, good and bad. It puts some people on the other side of a wall and fails to acknowledge their humanity. We separate ourselves from those we think are less than equal to ourselves and blame them for our societal woes. This side of ourselves often expresses itself even when we want to curb it.

Our views seem so obvious to us that we can't imagine how anyone could see things differently. Other people seem blind about the truth. Communication becomes difficult with those who seem out of touch with reality. But this view of others affects our ability to identify and work toward common goals and thus get our own needs met.

The more we limit our interactions only to those who we think are like us the less able we are to interact productively to make our lives and democracies work. This undermines the vision of equality essential to democracy. To preserve our democracies we must be able to engage in dialogue about a common direction without allowing our judgmental self to dominate our discourse and actions.

Fifty years ago strict segregation was practiced in the United States and South Africa based on what some believed was the obvious inferiority of one race. Segregation created a culture where people saw each other only as members of their group rather than as individuals. It resulted in separate economies – shops, schools, restaurants and even rest rooms – that had negative effects for both sides. Similarly, residents of some nations vilify immigrants while most studies show that the bulk of them make positive contributions to their communities and economies.[26]

Of course there are individuals who we cannot or should not trust. This includes those who have caused harm to us or others, or are repeatedly unreliable. They need to be avoided or even ostracized until they can demonstrate an ability to be responsible in their intent and actions. But how people act and who they are is not the same. Some actions are helpful to our world and make it a better place. Some actions are harmful or even treacherous, meriting isolation to protect society. Those whose actions threaten the social fabric lose our trust until they do what is required to restore it.

Each of us at some point has harmed others – intentionally or not. But nothing we or others have done makes us less human or less equal. Just as we see children as capable of being taught and retrained, we can view everyone as capable of retraining and rehabilitation. We all want forgiveness and compassion from others, yet often refuse to extend it to those we judge as less than equal to ourselves.

Our judgments are based on a limited view of others. Opening to a more complete understanding allows us to see people as individuals rather than as the labels we foist upon them. This is, of course, how we want others to see us. And just as we believe we don't deserve eternal condemnation, none of us are gods qualified to impose condemnation on others.

When we think that people criticize us, we put up a shell to protect ourselves from what we consider a personal attack and we often attack back to deflect what we perceive as a threat. Our focus – when we take these comments personally – becomes not what we have done or can do, but whether we are good or bad human beings.

We may at times become discouraged and assume that others – and the world – are against us. It is not what others think that affects us, but what we tell ourselves about what they think. Assuming that the world is critical, whether accurate or not, inhibits our effort at everything we try. But when we believe the world is supportive, it enhances our confidence and creativity and makes us more likely to deal success-fully with challenges.

The messages we receive verbally as children, or by watching those around us, set our standards for how to look, how to act, and what to believe. With time there are greater expectations placed on us for appro-priate behavior. If our intelligence is respected we learn confidence in our ability to set and achieve our goals.

Equality – and respect for others – can be brought into every encounter. We can make clear that we are not above or below others. It can be conveyed by a gesture, touch, or inflection of voice as well as by our words. As we recognize the individuality and value of others, we come closer to the truth of who they are while experiencing the recognition that we seek at the same time.

For those who support democracy, it is our com-mon humanity with each of the people on our planet that defines our purpose and clarifies our path. Our individual cultures also are a part of who we are and these can be brought into our interactions. But ulti-mately our interactions must reflect our allegiance to all of humanity if we are to sustain our planet and the human race. Some people operate under the illusion of individualism, but there are no "self-made" men or women. We all depend on others to survive.

Most of us believe that there are factors – genetic and environmental – that have made us the way we are.[27] We blame our upbringing, our circumstances or other people for our state of mind. But our anger – justified or not – always hurts us as it festers in our minds. Our complaints fail to lessen our discomfort. Others may not even be aware – or may not care – that they are being blamed. Dwelling on resentment keeps us from putting our energy in moving toward our goals.

An alternative is to allow ourselves to experience our feelings as they occur without blaming anyone or anything. We then provide ourselves the empathy we seek. We no longer need the recognition of others as we provide our own. This then allows us to move on to creative interaction with others and our world.

The essence of democracy is a meeting of minds and spirits that recognizes the validity – and equality – of each of us. As we do this we can move forward to create the laws, procedures and institutions that best meet our needs.

2. Politics and Government

KEY PRINCIPLE: *Politics and government that support democracy are based on the principle of human equality and advocacy for the common good.*

Democracy is all about one fundamental truth: the essential equality of every human being; the idea that no one is better than anyone else, or as stated by Abraham Lincoln, "The proposition that all (human beings) are created equal."[28] But despite much progress since the founding of the United States – the first modern democracy – the promise of equality remains largely unfulfilled in many nations that consider themselves democratic.

Although considered a beacon of human equality for its time, the US fell far short of implementing that principle for women and minorities. The Supreme Court at one time upheld slavery[29] and segregation.[30] Women won the right to vote only one hundred years ago.[31] Many worker protections and prohibitions on child labor were put in place only in the mid-twentieth century after long struggles.[32] Voting rights still are denied to some because of race,[33] immigrants who seek refuge are maligned, and people of minority religions

40

are told to return to their own countries.[34]

A main theme of democracy is balancing our own interests with those of others, our community, our country and the world. But doing this requires clarity on our part about our own best interests and how to pursue them.

We choose on an ongoing basis whether to make democracy a living reality in our personal, professional and political lives. We only can guarantee fair treatment for ourselves by moving toward equal treatment for all and by bringing greater respect for every human being into our interactions and institutions.

There are two impulses that have aided human evolution over time. One is our inborn "fight or flight" response that has guarded us against enemies and still has the potential to protect us.[35] To make our everyday functioning easier, this part of our nature discriminates between those we perceive as good or safe to be around, and those we consider bad or dangerous. It once helped us make quick decisions about who to trust and who not to trust. The downside is it impels us to automatically cast people into categories as we blind ourselves to the truth of who they are. We often see people as the labels we thrust upon them based on race, religion, appearance or financial status, rather than for their intrinsic worth.

With the enlargement of our social units from tribes to nations, we found that identification and cooperation with larger groups worked better for stability and long-term survival. We sublimated our aggressive impulses to cooperate with others toward a more safe and stable world. But our instinct to judge others never

41

left us. It still affects our everyday interactions and creates a gap between us.[36]

Our civilization progresses or regresses based on our actions. If it is to continue to progress we must work together to move past our polarity toward a political system that recognizes the value of everyone. Effective leaders inspire us to create policies and laws based on the idea that we all are equal. Leaders who promote divisions focus on stirring up enmity rather than identifying a vision for the future and forging a path forward. They endanger the progress – and lives – of everyone, including those who follow them.[37]

People vote for politicians and parties based on promises that often are not kept. But the most ardent followers continue to back their leaders regardless of whether their policies help or hurt their countries or even themselves. These followers allow themselves to be fooled by a continuing repetition of how "the other" stands in the way of their country's success. They are guided primarily by divisiveness which results in their own stagnation and that of their society.

Among countries that consider themselves democratic, the US was the first to be founded on a vision of revolutionary leaders who sought to overthrow tyranny. Its founders were able to work together and stay focused because of the threat at their door. But the hardest part for the leaders of the young country was determining how to protect their democracy once that threat was overcome. When their Articles of Confederation did not work to create a viable nation, they reconvened to forge a more comprehensive Constitution.

That Constitution, written in 1787, required four

months of negotiation and numerous changes. It was a compromise that provided a broad guideline for how best to maintain a democratic vision. But after all agreed on George Washington as the country's first President in 1789, unity was elusive. Even during his administration previous allies regressed into partisan feuding. They reverted to their tribal instinct to identify an enemy which made former friends into foes. That legacy of combat between politicians and political parties continues to this day.[38]

In the realm of politics we are more easily united by what we don't want then what we do want. The US founders knew they didn't want tyranny. Clarifying a direction for the young country via its Constitution was the political miracle of its time. Its legacy of human equality still is with us. Yet in everyday practice we often fail to honor this mandate. When people believe that not only their ideas are superior, but they also are as well as the groups with which they identify, it creates an unbridgeable gap. The essential truth of equality – that none of us are superior – clearly is stated in the US founding documents. Yet because of our tribal instincts many of us often ignore that principle in our personal and political interactions.

It is natural to align ourselves with those we consider like us and who think like us. But there is a difference between confronting ideas with which we disagree and attacking the individuals who state those ideas. When we attack others personally we impede our ability to move toward solutions. And when we take disagreements with others as personal attacks – whether intended or not – it distracts from our vision of moving toward greater equality. Instead we can respond with a larger truth – that democracy succeeds when guided by universal respect – in our words and actions. A pattern of continual attack and response prevents us from seeing the humanity of others and distracts us from our own. It creates polarity among ourselves, our political parties, and our nations. Assuming the worst about others distorts our communication and moves us further from finding a mutually agreeable path. A glimpse at the dysfunction of legislative bodies around the world – even in democracies – makes that clear.[39]

We each believe in the truths that we have developed over our lifetimes, but none of us has the entire truth. We often seek validation for ourselves before we are willing to trust others. But instead of waiting for validation, extending it toward others may be the first step to allow us to focus on solutions. When we put ourselves in the place of others we are more likely to understand their point of view and progress toward mutual understanding. We – and our legislators – can model respect toward each other by honoring differences of opinion without personally attacking those with whom we disagree.

We can learn from our history of having succeeded at times – and failed at times – to honor human equality. By definition the past is over, so – if we choose – we now can move forward by working via respectful interaction to create rules and laws that address how we best can protect the rights of all. Then our actions must be carefully reviewed and revised as needed to verify that we are upholding the democratic vision in our deeds as well as words.

Abandoning the principle of human dignity has led to dire consequences for the world's democracies. The assumption of superiority of some over others has resulted in countless wars. Many of these have been foisted by democracies on other nations. The US entered the Spanish American war of 1898 under the guise of ending the oppression of Cuba by Spain, then it imposed oppression on Cuba and other Spanish territories, including the Philippines. World War II was brought on by the ability of Hitler – who was democratically elected – to sell racial superiority to the Germans. The American war in Vietnam was sustained by continual mistruths about the war's progress while disregarding thousands of lost lives. The 2003 Iraq War was justified by false US claims of the possession of "weapons of mass destruction," which provided an excuse for a large power to impose itself on a smaller one.

A major issue for many of us is how to know what to believe among competing views presented by politicians, the media, government, and organizations. For many of us, the first thing we do in the morning – and the last thing at night – is check our favorite news source. We depend on our televisions, radios, computers, newspapers and personal devices. Often we seek the simplest explanation of events instead of introducing a healthy skepticism.

There is much talk in our society about what news is real and what is not. Many of us have a great distrust of media sources that we believe are aligned on the other side of the political divide from ourselves, often without actually watching or listening to them.

Media that best supports democracy presents a variety of views rather than telling us what to think. Personalities that start with the conclusions they want us to believe – and then repeat the same message continuously – are preying on the tribal part of our minds that want simple answers rather than truth. A source cannot be trusted that supports one person or party regardless of what they say or do. Responsible news reporters seek the truth and are open to the possibility that their stories are incorrect. Real news encourages us to examine many sides of every issue. Keeping our minds open as we evaluate our input is the responsibility of participants in democracy.[40]

To make democracy work we cannot simply believe the scenarios provided by the media, a political party, or even a book, including this one. We must seek many perspectives before we settle on our own, and then continue to be open to new information for our ideas to stay close to reality. For democracy to function as "government by the people" we must come to our own conclusions based on a balanced view of what we hear and what we see. This rarely is done as we become more partisan and less willing to consider that there may be a larger truth beyond the echo chamber of our minds. The truth of human equality that underlies democracy is our only reliable guide.

The promise of democracy is greatly diminished in many nations that once showed impressive progress. There is no exact moment when a country turns from a democracy to an oligarchy; when we move from supporting the interests of all to the interests of only a few. It's only when we look back after a period of decline that we realize that a transformation has taken place.[41]

After the fall of the Soviet Union in 1991, the constitution of Russia promised democracy. The satellite Soviet nations, such as Poland, Hungary and Lithuania also showed great promise. Around the same time, many nations in Central and South America created new constitutions that promised democracy. Former colonial nations from Africa to Asia – including Ivory Coast[42] and the Philippines – also stated their intentions to create greater equality among their citizens. But each of these countries have retreated from their promise and now dwells on the edge of oligarchy or a return to dictatorship.

Many of our current policies and laws also are based on ignoring the truth of human equality. The Citizens United Supreme Court decision of 2010 allows the wealthy to influence elections with unlimited funding. Drug laws in the US stigmatize the use of crack cocaine over the powdered version which puts blacks in jail up to 18 times longer than whites for using the same substance in a different form.[43] The promise of equal voting rights is diminished in many states that engage in voter suppression and gerrymandering. Limited employment opportunities for American natives who are forced onto reservations lead to alcoholism and suicide.

Political advocacy often is done effectively by non-governmental organizations representing those who consider themselves treated unfairly. These can be workers, teachers, environmental groups, citizens representing their cities or rural districts, leaders of small or large businesses, representatives of individuals with disabilities, or others. It is up to our elected officials to balance the interests of these groups as much as possible as they shape law and public policy.

Politics has the potential to bring us together to pursue common needs or to divide us. In our age of partisan politics, the word patriotism rarely is used because it no longer fits the raw partisanship that guides us. It is a term that has been used to threaten individuals and question their devotion to democracy's ideals. Real patriotism in democracies is a commitment to identify and move toward a shared vision of equality in a nation, not necessarily to promote its current form. Once tyranny is overthrown, patriots rally to preserve democracy by working together to identify and implement its vision.

The American experiment once was considered "a city upon a hill" for those who sought freedom.[44] Now we must ask how we overcome our polarization to make democracies more worthy of that label. That starts with a respectful conversation between those with similar views – and those with opposing views – based on democracy's core principles. The questions that are most essential to resolve are: (1) What are the most basic principles for those who believe in democracy? (2) What would following those principles look like? (3) How do we turn that vision into action? This will allow us to move toward greater agreement on the challenging path of the realization of our democratic vision.

3. Truth and Education

KEY PRINCIPLE: *Education that supports democracy emphasizes skills to move society toward a greater sense of human dignity and respect for the spirit of innovation.*

For most of the early human story, education was preparation for one's role as an adult by imitation of one's parents, based on local truths such as what and where to hunt, how to adjust to changing weather patterns, and where to forage. It was all the education children needed to fulfill their eventual roles as adults.

As our ancestors gained agricultural knowledge that improved their chance of survival, groups clashed in wars to expand their rule over others.[45] Each society educated its members in the knowledge required to sustain itself. Egyptians expanded to kingdoms and worshiped their Pharaoh as a God, while their education revolved around maintaining that truth. The ancient Greeks taught identification with the values of their individual city states – some were more democratic and some more autocratic – which led to conflicting values and war. The Romans created a rich civic life that rewarded those who became educated in the rules and laws of the state.[46]

In the East, particularly in China, there was an expansion of states often at war. People were taught beliefs needed for allegiance to their dynasties.[47] Education centered on the truths required to support their leaders and autocratic societies.

In Europe under Charlemagne, around the year 800, a great political consolidation took place. Education for those who were to serve the empire was emphasized to promote the religious and secular truths needed for its perpetuation.[48] When that empire deteriorated, education again became local until modern European states began to emerge hundreds of years later. It was the growing stability of those states that again promoted the truths – based on allegiance to their monarchs – that sustained expanding European kingdoms and their inhabitants.

In most of Europe up until the Middle Ages, the education that boys received was primarily in the skills of their fathers. Family crafts remained the same for generations. Girls learned the skills they would need to support a household.

In the 1100s and 1200s, children of the wealthy began to attend fledgling universities across Europe. The original intent of these universities was training in religious teachings and classics going back to the ancient Greeks, but eventually they emphasized a larger search for truth that included philosophy and science. With time, the monopoly of the Church on truth weakened as universities began to encourage scientific methods based on experiment and observation.

Growing commerce and a need for improved record keeping created a demand for knowledge of history, geography and mathematics to support the expanding economy, with universities emphasizing professions related to the merchant trades.[49] Trade became more extensive with better ship design and the importation of food and other items that were sent longer distances. As civilization advanced and prospered, so did the educational level of many to support that effort.

With the advent of the European Renaissance in the 1400s the predominant truth about the average working person in the West progressed from relative insignificance to being of value just because they were human – an idea that would come to be called humanism. There was a slow improvement in economic conditions for most, and an appreciation of the importance of education for a larger percent of the population.

This advancement, however, only applied to the European races. Others, such as Blacks and New World natives, often were removed from their ancestral homes to serve the expanding economy. They were considered inferior and not worthy or capable of being educated. Thus the benefits of European society were confined mainly to the Europeans themselves.

In the late 1500s, Michel de Montaigne wrote influential essays about the purpose of education as being primarily to guide us in our pursuit of truth: "Let him be taught to throw down his arms and surrender to truth as soon as he perceives it, whether that truth is born at his rival's doing or within himself from some change in his ideas." [50]

By the 1700s "Enlightenment" writers – including Locke, Rousseau, and Voltaire – began to advocate for a broader education to improve the human condition.

They envisioned a future in which people would be more free and have a right to overthrow oppressive rulers.[51] Medical training at universities and hospitals began to emphasize how the health of people could be improved via hygienic practices. The average lifespan increased.

But in most of the east of Europe and the Orient the predominant truth remained that people are subordinate to their ruler. Their educational systems were built around that belief. In Russia the authority of Father Tsar never was to be questioned. In China, books were burned to keep the population from having too much knowledge, and servants were buried with their masters when rulers were assumed to need help in the afterlife.

The promise of the New World – and then the American Revolution – brought an increasing emphasis on the value of the individual. Schools sprang up to educate youth of European ancestry, at least the males. The general thrust of Western civilization – and of the education needed to move it forward – continued to bring greater progress to most.

The New England colonies mandated public funding for educating children of age six and up beginning in the 1600s. The emphasis was on the basic reading, writing and math skills that were considered essential for a productive member of society. By the mid-1800s, free education laws were passed in eastern states such as Ohio and Pennsylvania, followed by a number of Midwestern states.

Along with an increased emphasis on the value of the individual in the United States, the purpose of education began to be addressed by some prominent educators. In the late 1800s John Dewey asked important questions about the role of education in preparing students for democracy. He believed that they must be taught to understand its core values and how to apply them in the context of the real world. He stressed that this type of education is needed to assume one's role in a democratic society.[52]

Robert Maynard Hutchins, at the University of Chicago after Dewey, proposed that an educated individual in a democracy must become familiar with ideas of the great thinkers of all time. This provides the basis of knowledge that modern democracy needs to sustain itself. These truths are best taught via interactive dialogue that respects the views of students as they are exposed to the most important tenets of civilization. Hutchins emphasized that the best way to understand the democratic process is by participation and practice. He believed that those who are well-grounded in democratic decision making are qualified to participate with confidence in any field.[53]

Education always has been – and always will be – centered on the truths held by the society to which one belongs. The skills needed by most primitive tribes revolved around their immediate needs, whereas in modern society we interact with a large network of people to meet our goals. As societies have expanded, so have their knowledge and grasp on the truth. But the progress of civilization is impeded by those focused only on their immediate truths because the demands of our times force us to work together toward a common vision.

In our day there are competing truths among

nations and conflicting educational systems to back them up. The trend toward greater recognition of human dignity that came out of the European Enlightenment resulted in a model of government that championed the value of human beings and their right to replace their rulers when oppressed. All democracies began elections after their revolutions. But in nations on all continents democracies have shown recent signs of declining along with their educational systems. Russia, among the most prominent recent examples of a failed attempt at democracy, has a standardized authoritarian educational system pre-approved by the state. Even in democracies, where the primary truth is the value of the individual, educational systems still struggle to keep up with how democratic values can best be taught.

This brings us to a crucial question. What is the purpose of education, particularly in democracies, and how does this relate to the pursuit of understanding and truth? Perhaps even more important: how do the insights imparted by our education effect our hopes and actions to preserve democracy for ourselves and the generations to follow?

Human beings are programmable. Our minds are set up to absorb information from the world around us and turn it into lessons that we apply in new situations.

When we begin formal schooling we seek approval from our teachers and absorb what we are told to learn and believe. We rarely question the truth of our early lessons because our self-esteem rests on whether we can duplicate and return the information we are given. Only the rare teacher or school trains us how to come to our own conclusions based on reflection about what we observe or learn from our interactions with the world.

The way children are educated – from their earliest schooling right up to college – goes hand in hand with the level of democracy in a country. If children are taught that they, and their attempts to explore the world around them, are to be honored – including the conclusions that result from that exploration – they are likely to understand what human respect and dignity are about. If education is about compliance with prevalent values or what we are told, original ideas will be quashed along with much of the creative impulse. In the former model, the prevailing truth is the dignity of the human being consistent with democracy. In the latter model, a genuine understanding of democracy is unlikely to take place because the underlying principle of human equality never is practiced.

An essential element of democracy is that there is no one single authority on what is true. The best path forward always needs to be worked out among us. But encouraging children to communicate with others and interact to reach their own conclusions is rare even in democracies. Talking and reading about democracy is not the same as experiencing it.

Traditional education values description above observation and experience. The essential emphasis of education in our society has become "Do what you're told and you will get a good grade," which, for those who learn that lesson, eventually translates to "Do what you're told and you'll get a good job." The danger to our political system is that this moves us in the direction of government officials and political parties who require loyalty to themselves rather than to the essential principle of democracy, which is valuing the needs of everyone.

Children are most likely to accept the narrative of those with whom they have a trusting relationship. Those who mentor them have a considerable responsibility for their future and that of their society. Rather than imposing our views and judgments, we can encourage students to learn to come to their own conclusions. This involves a long and patient process to train them to take a role as responsible participants in democratic interaction. If they make a mistake, rather than judging them, we can ask: "Well, did we learn anything from that?" If they are impressed with a film or book, rather than interpreting it for them, the question could be: "What do you think they are trying to tell us?" When discussing politics, rather than teaching children to take sides, we can ask: "What do you think could have been done better?" This emphasizes training in the independent thought and action needed to move students closer to democratic principles rather than loyalty to an authority figure or political party. It teaches the vital skills of thinking and communication that are essential to students as citizens in democracy.

The maintenance of democracy requires people who can review information – including a variety of sources – and come to their own understanding about what is true and what is not. The best teachers are aware that all conclusions are an expression of our current state of understanding and never absolute truth. They then pass this perspective to their students.

When we simply believe what we are told by

teachers or others, we give up our right to actively form our views, which is the essence of participation in the democratic process. The consequence of not training our children to develop their own views is the likely deterioration of democratic society itself.

Teachers must teach – and model – respect for those at all levels of society if children are to understand what it means that all are created equal. An education that prepares children for democracy is based on understanding the evolution of the truths that have governed us and how building on that knowledge can move our civilization forward.

The economies and lifestyles of people who live under democracies generally has excelled those of other systems, and that is no accident. An educational model that encourages innovation and confidence is likely to lead to new discoveries and inventions that benefit those at all levels of society.

Truths are not easily expressed; our ideas about the world develop slowly in our minds. Exposure to the world – and learning to reach our own conclusions – is more likely to lead to realistic and practical understanding than instruction in what is "true." Practice at coming to our own models about the world teaches us how to think. Then we need to see how our ideas work. We often will need to revise our concepts of what is true, with input from others, to implement them as they guide our actions. This should be included in our teaching techniques so as to optimize the potential of students to understand and succeed in the world.

Teaching children to come to their own truths can begin at an early age. Finland, which sits in the shadow of Russia, has been subject to a long history of propaganda from that neighbor. Their educational system starts with fairy tales for school beginners about the "sly words" of politicians being like those of a fox. In secondary schools, they instruct students in strong critical thinking skills to evaluate for themselves what they are told, and learn how easy it is to lie with statistics.[54] These efforts serve as a model for what can be done in all democracies to train students to look past what they are told and come up with a balanced version of truth.

For those open to the lessons that life holds for us, education is a life-long process. We continually learn from others and experience what works and what does not. Yet there is that place within us – the irrational or the tribal – that refuses to learn. It clings to what it thinks it knows rather interacting and learning from others and the world. But when we acknowledge this part of ourselves – rather than ignoring it – we find it less able to manipulate us.

As children learn and grow they especially thrive by having their creative impulses recognized as they gain in competence and confidence. They prosper as they construct their own understanding of the world which then affects their actions. They can be guided in learning how to think, but telling them what to think impedes their ability to be productive members of a democratic society. Those of us who want to see our democracies maintained must safeguard our educational systems to protect, rather than impede, the democratic impulse in every developing individual.

4. Truth and Economics

KEY PRINCIPLE: *The goal of economics in democracy is creating conditions that foster the greatest potential in every individual.*

Adam Smith was the founder of modern economics. His classic, *The Wealth of Nations* (1776), has been seized upon by those who prefer that governments operate with as few regulations as possible, claiming that an "invisible hand"[55] creates an economic climate that works best for all.

But Smith himself was not convinced that this view, which reduces human interaction to financial transactions, always is valid. He lamented that "For one very rich man there must be at least five hundred poor."[56] In his earlier work, *The Theory of Moral Sentiments* (1759) he described the importance of what today we would call empathy: "This is the source of our fellow-feeling for the misery of others, that in changing place in fancy with the sufferer, we come either to conceive or be affected by what he feels."[57] The suffering of others makes us uncomfortable. Those at all ends of the economic and political spectrum are aghast at the growing homeless epidemic on our streets.

The contrasting views expressed by Adam Smith

summarize what have been the main trends in economics ever since. Should our policies allow whatever the market brings, based on the assumption that it is self-regulating, or should an empathetic connection between people be factored into our strategies? Is it true that our separate interests automatically balance out for the best, or is consideration of another truth, that of our interdependence, most conducive to general prosperity?

To understand economics in an historical sense, we must begin by looking at periods long before the advent of money. In primitive times there was general equality within small tribes whose members worked together for the general good. Possessions were fewer and more evenly distributed.[58] As tribes expanded into nations, the distance between leaders and the average person increased. This was the case in Egypt, China, and every other known ancient civilization. At that point inequality between those who ruled and those who were ruled was considered normal.

In ancient Athens about 600 BCE, the inequalities resulting from farmers needing loans from the most wealthy members of society threatened economic stability due to great imbalances that led to some people losing everything. A resolution under Solon – known as the "law giver" – absolved these debts. Athens then became a place of greater equality and laid the foundation of democracy. Left on its own under the equivalent of the "laissez-faire" view espoused by many economists, Athens would have gone the direction of many other states toward entrenched inequality and oligarchy.[59]

The economic implication of the revolution by the

American Colonies during which they declared their independence in 1776 – the year of publication of *The Wealth of Nations* – was an emphatic rejection by the American founders of the policies of inequality, one of their truths being "that all (persons) are created equal." Ever since, in the United States and nations around the world – not all of them democracies – that same principle of human equality has been written into their constitutions.[60]

Modern economic policy is set by "experts" in a position of authority. They judge progress through their own eyes, as that which best serves them and those of a similar economic status. They often fail to view progress through the lens of those further down the economic scale. Economists tell us that their study of markets can improve economic conditions. But the field of economics often is about keeping the wheels of the economy turning while ignoring the plight of those stuck in the mud.[61]

After every revolution intended to overcome inequality, some individuals and their families rise to economic heights, while others are left behind. Russia, China, France, Venezuela, and the US are a few examples. Those with economic advantage – perhaps because of talent or luck – seek to maintain that advantage. Elections often result in a charismatic leader who promises greater equality but who actually puts policies in place that have the opposite result.

An example of how economic policy works can be found in the history of trade. Trade began long before there was money, first between tribes, then between individuals in town markets, and then at great distances, even in prehistoric times.[62] A large merchant class emerged in the Middle Ages that specialized in facilitating trade between city-states. Such is the stuff of the legend of Marco Polo. Merchants could make a handsome living if all went well. They drew investments from wealthy individuals via the likes of the Dutch East India Company and Hudson Bay Company. Governments enacted trade barriers to raise funds and protect their domestic producers.

In our day, trade agreements have been negotiated between nations on all continents, such as GATT, established after World War II (now the World Trade Organization), and NAFTA, between North American neighbors (now USMCA). But trade organizations, like every other international agency, can serve primarily those at the top or they can further the interests of those at all levels of the economy. When agreements are negotiated to allow "free trade" the results benefit companies, but trade agreements rarely have been negotiated with workers in mind. This has allowed companies to shop for the cheapest labor abroad while reducing the employment or pay of those doing similar work in prosperous countries.

But governments can negotiate trade agreements to protect workers by guaranteeing that they get a living wage and benefits. This promotes greater income equality and greater prosperity for everyone. When people at all levels of an economy have more to spend, it provides greater profits to businesses, who then can afford to pay higher wages. This has been the case in some periods of history, particularly after World War II, when there was growing general affluence for over thirty years. But after that, real wages in Western countries began to stagnate.[63] Government policies favored employers rather than employees.[64] Wages and benefits failed to keep up with inflation, and the new generation of workers and their families fell behind.

In many Western countries in the 1950s and 1960s, one person was able to work to support a family while the other stayed home to raise children. This allowed a family to have a house, car, medical benefits, retirement, and a chance for some children to advance themselves by going to college. Since that time, the level of real income (adjusted for inflation) has been declining for much of the middle class, even as both parents in most households began to work. Many families now forgo vacations, struggle with the costs of medical benefits, and have no idea of how they can afford to retire. College has become out of the question for those who have not seen economic advancement between generations. Many view themselves as treading water at best and in serious economic decline at worst. Meanwhile, corporate profits, and the income of the most wealthy, increase as a share in the growing economy is denied to millions.

Extreme inequality in a society impedes economic flow and negatively affects everyone. It has been repeatedly demonstrated that the closer we move toward prosperity for those at all economic levels, the greater the benefits for those at the top and bottom, as well as those in between.[65] If too much money is concentrated in the hands of a few, the bulk of consumers who support businesses have less to spend. If we care to simply observe the truth of what works and what does not work in economies the record is clear. When those at all levels are included in a growing economy, it benefits everyone. When policies favor only those at the top, the eventual result is a general decline.[66]

A couple of examples illustrate this point. Before the Great Depression that followed the 1929 stock market crash, there was a level of inequality not seen again until recent years. In the five years before that crash the stock market quadrupled. Many economists claim that market forces are rational because investors base investments on company profitability. But as happened before all crashes, the period before the Depression saw the stock market take off precipitously as a gradually greater number of people got involved. In financial markets people make what they think are the best economic decisions for themselves. But when everyone on a boat moves to one side the results can be disastrous.

The rise of the stock market during the 1929 bubble – and many others before and since – no longer was related to corporate profits. It became a frenzy that fed upon itself. The basis of the frantic rise was a spreading belief that nothing could go wrong. And then of course it did go wrong when the available money ran out. The government, not understanding that investment in a failing economy can contribute to saving it, at first enacted austerity measures that made the problem worse, spreading the contagion throughout the Western world.[67] Eventually legislators in the US limited speculation in investments by banks when they passed the 1933 Glass-Steagall Act that protected the economy for over 70 years.

Fast forward to the fall of 2008. Again in October,

the world economy was in a free-fall, beginning with the collapse of a bubble in real estate. When mortgages were left unpaid, it threatened to put banks out of business. Nine years earlier the US Congress and president had decided to undo the protections of the 1933 bank legislation. Banks again were able to speculate – with the money of their customers – on investments based on quickly rising real estate prices. This downturn was created primarily by providing mortgages to those who did not have the ability to pay them back. The irrational assumption of investors was that the real estate market would continue to rise beyond what people could afford. Those who brokered those deals made large commissions regardless of whether they were sound or likely to collapse.

There is another factor that can contribute to financial bubbles and the crashes that follow. The amount of money available in an economy is adjusted by governments to fit the needs of the nation. For example, the funds needed in the US at its founding were much smaller than what is required today when the country has roughly 100 times more residents. If there is too much money available it will put upward pressure on prices and threaten inflation. Too little money in circulation can lead to an economic pullback.

Taxes also affect the amount of money that consumers have available to spend. Higher taxes at times have contributed to less available money and a slowing economy, but tax cuts can result in too much available money, which can lead to higher prices and inflation. This hurts those whose incomes do not keep up.

In a growing economy, a greater money supply

supports increasing prosperity. If those at all levels benefit from a gradual economic boost, as happened in the years after the Second World War, prosperity is widespread, although there usually is some inflation due to pressure on prices. But if there is growing inequality, with the results of an improving economy going primarily to those at the top, an imbalance is created, like that leading up to the 1930s Depression and the 2008 Great Recession, that threaten the world economy.

The clear consequence of tax cuts benefitting primarily those at the top of the economic scale is greater inequality.[68] But people who believe themselves economically threatened will tend to vote for those who promise a way out of their plight. This is the source of mass discontent by voters that some term "populism."

The success or failure of an economy is based on the level of confidence of the public. If there is general optimism, markets tend to slowly improve. When confidence wanes, markets sink. Consumer confidence is positive when all or most are involved in a generally increasing prosperity. Polarities that negatively affect economies are created when some see themselves ignored by an economy that passes them by.

The way out? Both economists and politicians need to recognize the difficulties of those who see themselves as economically trapped, as many have been since the 2008 financial meltdown. These people need more than rhetoric. They need action by government to rekindle their engagement in the economy by the use of education, job training and other means – including public-private partnerships – that allow them to regain their dignity and confidence in their future.

There is one main reason why economies have succeeded in democracies and one main reason why they have failed. This is tied to the success and failure of democracies in general. In the words of Abraham Lincoln: "A house divided against itself cannot stand."[69] He was referring to the tragic polarity of North and South during the American Civil War, in which more lives were lost than any in US history. Both sides were convinced of the rightness of their cause; one economy built primarily on agriculture based on slavery, the other an industrial economy that provided poor wages and working conditions. The disruption of economic flow between the two contributed to lost markets on both sides while cotton rotted in the fields and manufactured goods from the north lost much of their market.

The key to prosperity is based on the economic truth we hold that then affects our actions. We each have two possibilities within us: a part that sees our interests as separate from others, and a part that under-stands that our interests are tied to the whole.[70] When we act on the first reality we contribute to an economic polarity that is in conflict with democracy and our own best interests. But when we support an economy that "lifts all boats," in the words of John F. Kennedy, we also contribute to our own security.

What benefits everyone also benefits each of us individually. In our economic and everyday pursuits we will be more likely to thrive as individuals if we work to clarify what works best to serve us all. In democracies the truth of human equality always is our best guide.

5. Truth and Science

KEY PRINCIPLE: *The mission of science in democratic nations is improving the standard of living for the bulk of their inhabitants.*

We begin life as enthusiastic explorers of our world. We formulate our ideas as we slowly learn the skills needed to interact with the people and objects around us.

As we age, we adopt more comprehensive views based on our experience and input from our parents, teachers, and friends. Longer periods of observation and interaction lead to greater understanding. But because there is a limit to the knowledge we can attain by our own experience, we created what we call science, which is based on shared observation.

The truths of our earliest ancestors were tied to their immediate needs. Before there was civilization, our focus was on finding herds and plants needed for food, how best to hunt, and how to build shelters. The discovery that food could be cultivated led to agriculture and advancement toward the sustainability of the human race.

Once people settled into towns and cities, scientific inquiry began to discover larger truths to provide insight into our world and cosmos. In ancient Egypt scientific minds discovered how to build the pyramids and embalm the dead.[71] Astronomers designed a calendar based on observation of the stars that predicted the annual flooding of the Nile.

The Greek philosophers speculated about the universe while creating the scientific theories of their time. Aristotle's teaching that motion is caused by the interaction of the four elements of earth, water, wind and fire was considered to be how the world worked for nearly 2000 years. Archimedes used mathematics to explain natural phenomena and invented practical inventions to demonstrate his ideas. Pythagoras made discoveries in geometry that still are used. The advantage of the conciseness of mathematics over ordinary language became more accepted to enhance functional knowledge such as masonry.

In the late 1500s Galileo overthrew the ancient truth of Aristotle that bodies fall with velocities proportional to their weights. He discovered that all objects fall at the same velocity, contrary to what many considered common sense. He also challenged the Aristotelian orthodoxy that the earth is the center of the universe. The church only was temporarily able to censor that new truth.[72]

Theories continued to be developed that advanced our understanding and overthrew what we thought we knew. In the 1600s Newton demonstrated that the trajectory of a moving body could be predicted by knowing its mass, existing motion, and the forces acting upon it. This and his other discoveries were considered absolute truth for over two hundred years.

But even in that era of scientific experimentation, theories not based on evidence remained in common use. Scientists in the 1700s maintained that an element called *phlogiston* is contained in all combustible bodies and released during fires. Up until the 1800s, "humors" in the blood were believed to be needed in proper balance to maintain health, and that an imbalance could be resolved by bloodletting.

Theorists of every period – both ancient and modern – were convinced that their latest ideas were the truth. But no scientific framework – up to and including our own – is the truth itself. Our theories only are the best concepts of reality that our minds are able to create based on our interpretation of the evidence before us. As we make new discoveries, we look back at old theories as being incomplete at best and foolish at worst, as people no doubt will when they look back at our own time.

Our perceptions are affected by a "critical mass" of information. Our conclusions often are based on where we look. When we gaze at a rosebush we see beauty if the bulk of flowers look healthy. When we examine the world for scientific truths, we seek beauty in the descriptions and formulas we use to interpret our observations. Because of this we easily can overlook evidence that contradicts what we want to believe, and this occurs outside of the realm of science as well.

Advancing theories based on observation and experimentation has moved us forward toward better explanations of the world over time. This has led to a view in every period of history that everything about the universe already has been, or will be, explained.

70

Yet a complete understanding never has been reached despite the efforts of our greatest scientific minds, and we are unlikely ever to do so because there always is more to reality than our minds can envision.

In 1905, a young customs clerk studying on his own superseded the established truths of Newton's mechanics. Einstein's relativity theories – both special and general – set the world of physics on fire because they accounted for events that classical mechanics could not, including the view of an individual moving in relationship to others and the constancy of the speed of light from every perspective. His primary revelation was that: "...our concepts and laws of space and time can only claim validity insofar as they stand in a clear relation to our experiences...."[73] He basically overthrew the idea of objectivity in science. General Relativity also predicted the existence of black holes that occur when massive stars collapse, creating a spiral that twirls and eventually sucks in everything around it. Einstein perhaps is most famous for the idea that matter and energy are identical ($E=mc^2$). As relativity shook the world of science, many thought it was the final word.

But not long afterwards, in the mid-1920s, the developers of quantum mechanics theorized that, at least at the level of the atom and electron, particles only move in minimal "quanta," and that particles of light also could behave like waves. The quantum was the smallest possible unit of light that had been described in 1900 by Max Planck. According to the quantum theorists, if one were to track the location of a subatomic particle it would be impossible to describe its path, and in tracking its path one would not be able to determine

71

its position. After initially noting the location of an electron, the observer could not apply causality, but only could determine the probability of the next position in which it would be found. A description of the smallest units of matter could be in terms of their position or their movement, but not both, a view that Neils Bohr called "complementarity."[74] As mysterious as quantum theory seems, it has allowed for the development of lasers and modern electronics. Yet because of its inability to provide certainty, it was not the complete theory sought by Einstein and others.

Much of the efforts of physicists since that time have been devoted to discovering the "theory of everything" – the unifying concept that ties all other theories of the universe together. Stephen Hawking was probably the most well-known theorist who attempted to combine the insights of relativity and quantum mechanics. In opposition to the view that there is one unfolding universe, the "many worlds" concept that he supported is that there may be an infinite number of universes hidden to our view.

String theory, touted by physicist Brian Greene and others, also proposes that there are numerous universes. According to these theories, even beneath atoms and electrons are quarks. String theorists hold that at the unseen level are vibrating strings or connections, rather than particles, that determine the basic nature of the cosmos at the submicroscopic level, and that these are windows to other universes.[75]

One of the perennial questions of science is why does the universe exist at all. Is creation an accident or a planned event?

Ancient philosophers and most scientists until recently held that the universe is a cosmological constant, with no matter created or destroyed. But the observations of Edwin P. Hubble in Southern California created a revolution in cosmological theory by demonstrating in 1929 that our universe is expanding, and therefore must have begun in a single spot about four billion years ago with a "big bang." This theory was welcomed by many who held that if the universe had a beginning, there must have been a force that had a hand in creating it.

The question still remains why the universe is not simply composed of random particles. How did they organize themselves into what we recognize as matter? One theory that has been proposed by Lawrence Kraus and others is based on "virtual" particles that pop in and out of existence according to the rules of quantum mechanics and are responsible for the existence of matter.[76] Another theory that has been proposed is the Higgs Boson, originally developed by Peter Higgs and collaborators in 1964, that postulated why elementary particles have mass and have built up to the level of diversity and life that includes you and me. This idea, which is similar to a template upon which matter is built, is believed by many to have been confirmed in experiments at the Large Hadron Collider in Switzerland in 2012.

Our current idea of how the universe expands includes the theory of "dark matter" that has yet to be observed, but is assumed by many scientists to fill in the space as everything around us expands. Yet at some point if a better theory comes along, "dark matter" may prove to be one those unobserved placeholders in scientific theory – like phlogiston – that just didn't work out.

Our quest for truth is largely affected by what we expect to find. Many great scientific discoveries were preceded by a hunch that eventually panned out, although many hunches were followed by years of experimentation, such as in the invention of the light bulb by Thomas Edison.[77] When an idea seems likely to yield results, research or a theory often is developed in that direction. The great theories of a Marie Curie or an Einstein began as an inspiration about what new direction discoveries may lie, rather than a simple unfolding of the evidence before them.

Our discoveries have enhanced our survival and made our lives easier, with the possible exception of technologies that were developed to wage war. We have sought greater and deeper truths as we moved beyond philosophy to observation and experimentation that can be verified by repetition. We have superseded the understanding of each generation with the advent of the next, and many believe that we are close to an ultimate truth that can be reflected in a unified theory of our universe with practical implications for the improvement of our planet and lives.

But the applications of science also must match the realities of each era. We currently need science to take its role in introducing innovations that make our planet more livable. Perhaps some day we will have non-polluting cars that avoid accidents while taking us where we want to go based on a verbal command, plastic that self-destructs, and a way to pump cooling gasses into the atmosphere.

What may be missing in our hope for the perfectibility of our theories is the possibility of the perfectibility of the minds that hold those theories. We only can understand our universe by means of the apparatus we have been given. Even our fantasy that our concepts ultimately are perfectible may indicate an inner weakness. The consequence of believing that we can scale the heights to the level of ultimate understanding may very well be that great fall portrayed by the traditions of many cultures.

Perhaps instead we should view our scientific progress as part of a movement toward greater understanding of ourselves, as well as our world and universe. Perhaps the complexity of the universe is beyond the comprehension of the limited minds we bring to the task. Perhaps as our understanding deepens so will our appreciation of our limits. And perhaps we will gain greater humility as we realize that these built-in limits only allow us to get so close. With this realization our appreciation for the force that caused it all only will deepen.

To quote Werner Heisenberg, one of the great quantum physicists and the man who gave us the uncertainty principle: "It will never be possible by pure reason to arrive at absolute truth."[78] Perhaps it is best to see the truth we have as the framework in which we must function as we progress toward the next level of understanding.

6. The Environment

KEY PRINCIPLE: *In democracies the environment is considered an essential part of our support system that must be protected.*

We are our environment and our environment is us.

We believe ourselves separate from our surroundings because of an idea of the self; but that self eventually must return to its source.[79] Denying our connection to the world around us – both natural and human – has resulted in actions that endanger our environment and ourselves.

Acknowledging the truth of our effect on our quickly warming planet – now recognized by the vast majority of scientists and 75% of the population – or ignoring this truth, will determine the ability of our civilization to survive.[80] Inevitably our lives will be altered, either by making the needed changes, or by circumstances that soon will be out of our control. A simple truth is that we can't see climate change. A larger truth is that its evidence is everywhere if we believe what science has to tell us.

No matter what we do, our world – in one form or another – will survive until that time when the sun has burned itself out, perhaps five billion years from now.[81] But the future of our civilization is uncertain. Perhaps we who call ourselves Homo sapiens – or "wise" – will make the emergency adjustments needed for Earth to sustain itself. But if we fail to maintain the life-sustaining environment we have been given, new species may evolve suited to a planet overtaken by rising seas and drastic climate extremes.

Our planet is a living, breathing, multifaceted entity of which we only are a part. It is not a plaything in our hands, but rather the opposite – it is an ongoing expression of the original creation of which we will be privileged to be a part only as long as we study and honor it. When we try to bend it to our will it snaps back in revenge. It demands that we follow its laws rather than imposing ourselves upon it.

Human equality – though a truth in itself – is part of the larger truth that we all are interconnected with each other and our environment. Thus treating all of our surroundings with respect is the same as treating ourselves with respect. We are able to live only as we remain connected to our sources of food, air and water as well as to other people, and cooperate toward keeping our world viable. When we ignore our connections our source of life is threatened.[82]

Our environment also reflects our state of mind. When we focus on a part of our surroundings we see only that piece of the truth. When we expand our focus to take in a larger perspective a more comprehensive understanding comes into view. The complete truth always is – and always will be – beyond our limited minds. But as we open to a larger reality our comprehension expands as does our range of possibilities for action.

In our earliest times we saw ourselves as part of our environment. The resources we used – as well as our bodies – were returned to the earth. As we began to believe ourselves separate from the natural world we came to see it as a threat. Our relationship with our environment deteriorated as we plundered it for resources to support our increasingly complex lifestyles.

We live in a fishbowl. Every natural resource we use creates waste. Burning fossil fuels such as coal and oil adds to the stagnant greenhouse gasses surrounding the earth which warms the planet. This causes seas to rise and get warmer, threatening coastal cities and aquatic life. Taking fish and mammals from the sea and earth without regard to their depleting numbers threatens them with extinction. Plastics derived from oil are nearly indestructible while polluting beaches and oceans, choking birds and killing marine life. Fertilizers and pesticides we use to enhance crops leach into the soil and run down into our water supply. Even the methane expelled from cattle and from warming polar caps releases gases that lodge in the atmosphere and threaten our planet with increased warming.

This causes glacier ice to melt, flooding low-lying areas all over the world, especially during storms of increasing frequency due to our warmer atmosphere. Warming results in increasingly greater droughts that affect land struggling to support crops with food shortages in a time of worldwide population growth. Due to interruption or destruction of their habitats, reduction of species also affects the human food chain.[83] The poorest among us, who live close to the land and have little protection against the ravages of nature, are the most likely to suffer.[84]

Other areas of environmental neglect add to our danger. Lead from antiquated pipes leaches into public water systems, most notoriously in Flint, Michigan, but this problem is widespread.[85] Toxic weed killers, such as glyphosate, poison farmworkers and leach into our food and water.[86] "Forever chemicals" in everyday products contribute to increased cancer risk.[87]

As less developed nations adopt a more advanced lifestyle, they also contribute to the destruction of Earth's natural resources. They burn non-renewable fuels and plunder the earth and seas to catch up with the world's major economies.

No one knows for sure why the Mayans disappeared from the Yucatan Peninsula in what is now Mexico around the year 900.[88] They possessed advanced technologies including a complex written language, astrology and calendar-making.[89] Nature moved quickly to shroud what had been one of the most sophisticated civilizations on Earth, obscuring an extensive network of cities that only have been partially uncovered.

About 1500 miles north of the Yucatan are the remnants of the largest North American Native American settlement. The Cahokia Mounds culture, in Southern Illinois, disappeared in about the year 1300, also for unknown reasons, although members of area tribes continued to dwell nearby. Theories include the possibility that it may have declined due to difficulty in feeding its growing population, an inability to dispose of human waste, deforestation, severe floods, or disease transmission.[90]

Cultures can disappear due to gradually becoming more insensitive to the warning signs around them. This can happen because people don't want to change lifestyles, or because of leaders who fail to acknowledge the truth or make contingency plans to address encroaching disaster.[91]

In democracies we can make choices that limit environmental destruction and force our leaders to adopt Earth-friendly policies. Of course international cooperation also is needed.[92] But we even are reversing previous environmental progress in some places. Countries that consider themselves democratic recently have elected leaders who have de-emphasized environmental concerns, including Brazil, Australia, and the United States, which dropped out of the 2015 UN Paris climate agreement.[93] The US has rolled back over 80 environmental regulations in recent years.[94]

People are afraid of change, especially when they believe it will affect their livelihoods. If we are to communicate for the common good, we must acknowledge the humanity of those with whom we agree and also those with whom we disagree on environmental issues. We must stop picking winners and losers in our strategy to combat climate deterioration if we are to get the vast majority onboard. Poor areas are less protected but ultimately we all are threatened. It is essential to move quickly because the science is clear that global warming will create such drastic problems on Earth in the immediate future that the problem will be irremediable.[95]

The old technologies – heating systems, man-ufacturing and engines run on coal and oil – are the primary cause of our emerging global meltdown. We must commit ourselves to replace them with renew-able technologies such as solar or wind and even newer sources not yet in place or perhaps not yet invented. Those whose livelihoods are threatened can be trained in the newer technologies that will stabilize their lives and our planet. Legislation to support this transition will benefit the earth and everyone on it.

Not all solutions once considered revolutionary have worked out. For example, nuclear power plants have melted down and essentially become obsolete as the indestructible waste from spent fuel cells has been found to be unwelcome wherever governments have tried to deposit them.

There are many ways we can rebuild our planet while making our lives more economically secure. A number of proposals allow us to protect the environ-ment while creating jobs in the process. They have the potential to bring everyone into the effort to cre-ate earth-sustaining technologies that also promote human skills development. Our government, which now provides subsidies for polluting industries,[96] [97] can shift its priorities to the technologies of the future. We also can extend a hand to those parts of the world that lack resources to help them move in a sustainable direction, and whose pollution, not bound by borders, affects everyone.

As the world's democracies were forced into World War II we were ill-prepared for the battles ahead, with a limited array of ships, tanks and planes to take on the advancing fronts in Europe and Asia. Nevertheless, we were inspired by outstanding leadership to create an unmatched arsenal to battle the most extensive war in history. The current stakes are nearly as urgent. Our planet quickly moves toward being uninhabitable. Some examples of what is needed in our war to protect our planet lie below.

(1) **Commit to clean energy in heating, industry and transportation**. We are on the verge of clean energy with the spread of renewable wind and solar energy sources.[98] But our progress is slow. Governments can provide grants or tax breaks for companies that help expand our renewable energy consumption to 100% in ten years. Since our current grids are powered by a mix of clean and dirty sources, support can be provided for companies that speed us toward renewables in record time, just as we did by necessity during World War II. The potential for job growth in training in the renewable energy industry is unlimited.

(2) **Rebuild our crumbling infrastructure with sustainable building methods**. Much of our pollution and blight is from the deterioration of buildings, roads, bridges and other structures as they wear out and are deposited in landfills. Just the creation of concrete is a major source of air pollution. Steel from autos and other sources are strewn in junkyards, and using these scraps in new structures can reduce energy use. Many materials can be recycled and reused, but this will require encouragement and grants from government. Efficient building design that limits energy use

also is crucial.[99] This will move us in the direction of well-paying jobs that contribute to improving our environment.[100]

(3) **Protect and rebuild our water supply and infrastructure**. Floods and droughts have been with us since biblical times, but scientists tell us that they are increasing due to global warming.[101] An improved infrastructure that also would create jobs could include building levees to prevent or limit water damage in areas near oceans and rivers. As more areas are prone to droughts, our storage of the water that nature provides is woefully inadequate. Building cisterns under our streets – similarly to what the Mayans used but on a much larger scale – would make a great deal of water available that nature already provides but currently is allowed to literally wash away.[102] Again, this would create jobs. But our storage system could not be allowed to interfere with a healthy water flow that cleanses waterways and provides habitats for fish and other wildlife.

(4) **Address the plastics epidemic**. Plastic pollution increasingly affects our roads, parks, streets, schools, trails and homes. It lodges in the stomachs of fish, birds and whales, while washing up on our beaches. It is a convenience we seemingly cannot live without. But there has been significant movement toward creating plastics from corn and other substances that are biodegradable. The challenge is making plastics that are strong enough to not leak their contents but that still will reliably deteriorate over time. Degradable plastics

is another industry that we should subsidize with loans to entrepreneurs, which also will create jobs.

The goal for our societies from the beginning has been increased security in areas such as food, clothing and shelter. In parts of our world we have succeeded beyond what we have dreamed, while other areas lag behind. But with our success has come increased pollution and defilement of our planet along with alienation from the environment that we still need to protect for it to sustain us. Our missteps have come back to haunt us in the morass of waste we have created that now surrounds and saturates us. We are the inhabitants of a toxic stew of our making.

We once justified this by telling ourselves a story that this all is progress. But such progress has brought us to the brink of global deterioration. We need to regroup and refocus on sustainable lifestyles and industries that allow us to redefine our idea of progress as restoring our balance with the natural world to which we were born and which has borne us. Then we can be confident that we most likely will extend our existence until the party ends based on forces outside our control rather than our own self-destruction.

7. Health

KEY PRINCIPLE: *In democracies equal access to healthcare is seen as an essential right.*

As I write, the worldwide coronavirus pandemic (COVID-19) is circling the globe. Such viruses can jump from animals to people who are in close contact and then be passed easily among people.[103] This was the case with the 1918 bird flu pandemic that killed about 50 million people worldwide, including my grandfather, and the Ebola virus that broke out in the last quarter of the twentieth century.[104]

Such outbreaks only can be treated successfully by the efforts of governments working together under the guidance of their scientific communities. When public health decisions become political by trying to make politicians look good rather than admitting the difficulties involved and bringing all possible resources to bear, the results can be disastrous. This was the case with the response of the American government to Hurricane Katrina that struck the Gulf Coast in 2005.[105] During world-threatening epidemics, governments must be prepared – they must be able to anticipate and quickly assess the threat, which can result in timely action.[106] Hiding the truth of the severity of the situation interferes with adequate planning and invariably makes the outcome worse.

The severity of this initial outbreak in China was hidden – at first from the Chinese people and then from the world – according to world health experts.[107] Hiding the truth in non-democratic countries about a situation that might embarrass the government is routine, but this makes it much more difficult to plan and take action. If the outbreak had been confirmed earlier, cautionary measures such as quarantines and travel restrictions could have been put in place and perhaps a vaccine process started, saving many lives.

Countries need an infrastructure and expertise to manage mass health emergencies and must have spokespersons who can provide the public with accurate information about what to expect. As the coronavirus spread into Asian countries, many announced plans for serious precautionary measures to limit its effects. South Korea was ready and tested hundreds of thousands. Australia and New Zealand put immediate emergency measures into place. However, because of reduced staffing at the US Center for Disease Control and a revolving door at the US Office of Homeland Security, there was little competence at the top to comfort the public and provide accurate information as the threat mounted.[108] The US president cut the budget for disease preparedness and contradicted his own experts[109] about the likely spread of the disease, including about the time that would be required to develop a vaccine.[110]

History is marked with plagues, including the Black Death that wiped out one third to one half of Europe's population in the 1300s, devastating terrified individuals from all walks of life and what had been an improving economy.[111] No matter how advanced our medical techniques become, there always is some new scourge waiting to attack us. This is why we must continually be alert – with resources ready – to confront the next challenge that nature presents.

The coronavirus crisis will pass and a vaccine be developed after a long period of emotional and financial chaos. Life will return to routine and the financial markets again will begin to function normally. But what will we have learned from this epidemic? The preparedness of some countries which are ahead of Western nations in this area may serve as a model, including some in Africa, such as Nigeria, which has extensive experience dealing with Ebola.[112]

Contagions don't choose their victims based on economic status, race, religion or political affiliation. Like natural disasters they strike at random, never respecting the sanctity of life. When we make healthcare dependent on one's ability to pay, we are threatening the health of those at all levels of the economic scale. Protecting all of us is the only way to protect any. But in the latest period for which studies were done, health care coverage, at least in the US, has declined, largely due to an administration hostile to the country's health safety net, the Affordable Care Act.[113]

Public awareness of healthy lifestyles has made us more informed and generally healthier over time. Smoking now is banned in nearly all public areas in the US and many other countries. Exercise has become routine among many adults. It is fashionable to eat plant based diets and less fat. Most people have become aware of the connection between cleanliness, personal hygiene, and health, while food safety standards have improved.[114] There has been a worldwide drop in child mortality rates and deaths of women in childbirth, as well as a reduction in deaths from malaria, and an increased average life expectancy in most countries.[115]

However, many are dying earlier than their natural life span because of unhealthy – and often destructive – lifestyles. Despite the rising retirement age, the life expectancy in the US is declining.[116] Many people are becoming immobile at an earlier age. Experts think this is due to lifestyles that include excessive amounts of fat and refined sugar.[117] This has led to an obesity crisis as well as an increase in Alzheimer's disease. The suicide level also has increased along with drug overdoses from opioids.[118]

Stress can be a factor in poor health. People living in low-income areas plagued by crime often feel chronically unsafe and suffer a higher level of physical ailments. Studies have found that when people move out of stress-inducing environments they experience less lifestyle-related health issues such as obesity and diabetes.[119] A study also found that a chronic worrying pattern leads to stress-related health issues, and that hopelessness can make one's symptoms worse.

Most of us have noticed that our bruises and cuts were made to feel better when our mothers showed concern or provided sympathy for our injuries. The actual injury may not have been improved by mom's attention, but our view of it definitely did. Our focus moved from worry to a belief that we would be healed as the injury took up less of our attention and we experienced a nurturing connection with another human being.

In *Lost Connections,* Johann Hari challenges the view that our moods are merely chemical expressions of our brains that can be fixed by medication. He questions the need for the huge industry in Prozac and other depression drugs. He explores the attitudinal and environmental aspects of depression and insecurity. Hari claims that some of our negative feelings may come from comparing our lives with an unattainable ideal state: "There is a part of us that thinks: 'If I keep buying more stuff, and I get the Mercedes, and I buy the house with the four garages, people on the outside will think I'm doing good and then I can will myself into being happy.'"[120] He believes that much of our malaise is from continually trying to get ahead of others, which creates loneliness and isolation: "It turns out that…in most cases, loneliness preceded depressive symptoms."[121] The solution? "To end loneliness, you need other people – plus something else. You also need…to feel you are sharing something with the other person, or the group, that is meaningful to you."[122]

In *Never Enough*, Judith Grisel, a neuroscientist specializing in drug addiction, says that insecurity and loneliness can lead to addiction: "Longing for other, for something else, is at the core of my experience of self… From where or what I seek escape I can't say…"[123] The current opioid epidemic has claimed many lives: "Addiction today is epidemic and catastrophic...about a quarter of all deaths are attributed to excessive drug use. Worldwide, addiction may be the most formidable health problem…In purely financial terms, it costs five times as much as AIDS and twice as much as cancer...close to ten percent of all health expenditures go toward prevention, diagnosis and treatment of people suffering from addictive diseases...excessive use is remarkably common, cutting across geographic, economic, ethnic, and gender lines."[124]

We are more than just our bodies. Our health is tied to whether we feel valued as human beings and thus take care of ourselves, as well as our inner sense of optimism or pessimism. If our values always are competitive – getting ahead or doing better that those around us – we may be plagued by insecurity and stress that can take a toll not only on our minds but on our bodies. And much of our insecurity – particularly as we age – stems from whether we have adequate medical coverage to deal with infirmities that inevitably come upon us.

There have been numerous studies showing that taking care of ourselves affects our longevity and enjoyment of life as we age. Maintaining positive social relationships influences our self-esteem, which in turn affects our self-care.[125] Activities that challenge our brains keep our mental faculties functioning.[126]

As all areas, in the field of health – advanced as our techniques may have become – there is much more to be discovered. The best resource in health issues always is a wide range of committed individuals with varying expertise who can come together as a team. A leader who considers himself above seeking multiple resources – especially in a crisis – invites disaster upon those he purports to lead. The truth always remains beyond us – one step ahead of even our most sophisticated understanding.

As emphasized throughout this work, the welfare of every human being is intertwined. Risks to our health don't stop at community gates or international borders. That is why wealthy nations must support poor nations in dealing with health emergencies. One commendable example was the George W. Bush administration's HIV funding for Africa.[127]

Our own health and that of our families is inexorably connected to the health of everyone. Research into ways to improve our health and prevent epidemics only can be done successfully on a scale that exceeds the resources of any one nation. International cooperation is required to make progress in improving the health of everyone. The more we understand this – and the further we move toward that model – the healthier we will be.

8. Religion

KEY PRINCIPLE: *Religious freedom in democracies is the right to develop our own values and not to have the values of some imposed on others.*

Why have people participated in religious practice going back into prehistory? Does a God – or gods – really exist who holds sway over our lives? Is there a truth contained in religion that is not available to science?

The role of religion is to provide insight into the force that created the universe and to enhance our relationship with that force. Members of all major world religions follow ancient teachings that continue to inspire billions worldwide. Many find religion attractive because it offers a better version of truth than any of the other versions they know.

In his classic *Varieties of Religious Experience,* William James stated that to understand the basis of religion: "We must make search…for the original experiences which were the pattern-setters to all this mass of suggested feeling and imitated conduct."[128] In other words, what are the essential insights of those who inspired our religions and how would they like us to live based on their teachings?

All religions have their versions of the Creation Myth: "In the beginning is perfection, wholeness. This original perfection can only be...described symbolically...it can be conceived in the life of mankind as the earliest dawn of human history, and in the life of the individual as the earliest dawn of childhood."[129] Can we conceive of a time before the existence of the universe or even ourselves? Perhaps more importantly, why are we here, and do our religions provide an answer to that question?

In all times there have been prophets who have claimed intimate knowledge of divine truths hidden to most of us. Among these have been the shamans of tribes and the seers who represented the gods such as the Oracle at Delphi in ancient Greece.

Throughout history religions have been tied to the political leadership of their societies. In ancient Egypt the pharaohs were considered gods, although this was temporarily altered by Akhenaton, who initiated worship of the Sun God. Athens was named for the goddess Athena, and her temple was built on the Acropolis overlooking the city. The Roman emperors sponsored the state religion with its pantheon of gods derived from the deities of Greece, with some rulers claiming to be gods themselves.[130]

What became the Hebrew Torah originated around 1400 BCE[131] as an oral tradition that later was inscribed on scrolls. It chronicled the direct inspiration of God to Moses to convey the wisdom and laws that followed from those insights. According to the New Testament, Jesus reinterpreted the message of that tradition for his time and all time after. The message revealed to

Muhammad around the year 600 AD was designed to inspire the other "people of the book" – Jews and Christians – to reinterpret the insights of their prophets. His followers quickly spread the Koran throughout the Middle East, and they only were prevented from conquering Europe in the year 732.

The early Jews and Christians were persecuted by the Romans because they advocated for a god – and a truth – outside of the state-sponsored religion. But the emperor Constantine later recognized the growing power of Christianity, making it the state religion at the Council of Nicaea in 325AD. He then converted to Christianity before he died.

Throughout both Eastern and Western Europe for over 1,000 more years, Christianity was the state religion that dominated half the known world. As Christianity became the persecutor, many who rejected the view that Jesus was both man and God were persecuted, exiled or killed. This included Jews, Muslims, and even Christian sects, such as the Cathars of Southern France.

In the great religions of the Far East a different truth about the relationship between God and human beings evolved. The Indian Vedas, developing orally around the time of the origins of the Hebrew tradition, eventually were compiled in written form to convey the insights of the great Indian sages. They culminated in the revelation of the Buddha regarding the unity of all creation. Buddhism is an attempt to become liberated from the suffering inherent in the human condition by steadfast meditation and devotion to overcoming our mental bonds to the material world.[132]

The ultimate goal of Hinduism is the unity of the individual with the universe after many incarnations. The One is worshiped through divinities that represent many aspects of the universe, such as Shiva, creator and destroyer of all things, and Vishnu, preserver of forms. The Bhagavad-Gita, the most well-known of Hindu texts, composed in perhaps the first century BCE, is the story of Krishna, a divinity who came to earth to teach humans to bring a godlike consciousness into everyday life.[133]

The teachings of Confucius, who died in 479 BCE, are about perfecting one's actions in this lifetime based on dedication to ancient tradition. Truth and wisdom are to be found in devotion to studying and following the morality inherent in the past.[134]

Billions of people across the planet hold to the version of truth they find implicit in their religion. What they have in common is a belief that there is a larger truth outside everyday understanding that can be revealed by devotion to the practices of their tradition and that connecting with that truth – individually or through an intermediary – can bring us greater understanding of our place in the universe.

Within every religion there are both those who think that their truths are superior to others and those more tolerant of other beliefs. Thus religion can be used to justify tolerance or intolerance. Those who are less tolerant insist on strict adherence to the truths they claim represent their God. They often believe that those of alternative views are not deserving of respect or even life. Those who are tolerant have a forgiving God by whose truths they try to live. The consequence of intolerance is a world that is less functional due to discord. The consequence of tolerance is a world that functions more effectively due to respectful interaction with others.

Our tolerance or intolerance is determined more by choice than the dictates of belief. Much of the strife, war and slaughter throughout human history has been caused by those who believe that they must follow leaders who represent God on earth regardless of what they teach or where their teachings lead. Despite the admonition in the Bible – at the cornerstone of the major Western religions – to "have no other gods," these followers, which exist in branches of all major religions, have turned their leaders into gods.

The US founders, some of whom were religious and some not, were among the first to confirm that freedom of religion – and freedom to have no religion – must necessarily be guaranteed to all if anyone is to be free. According to Thomas Jefferson, a "wall of separation" between church and state is required if the freedom promised by democracy is to survive. The first amendment to the US Constitution states: "Congress shall make no law respecting an establishment of religion, or prohibiting the free exercise thereof." Thus intolerance based on religion has no place in true democracies.

Those who support the essential values of Western religions – and democracy – as summarized in the Golden Rule, acknowledge the value of every human being while rejecting the views of those who do not. Those who believe that theirs' are the only viable truths often accuse others of intolerance because they live in a world that projects and mirrors intolerance.

If there is a creator who placed us on earth, then that creator likely values all of the creation. Or perhaps we are the result of a random eruption that formed our universe four billion years ago in a continually expanding event that has cascaded forward since that time. Either narrative leads to the view that no human being is superior to any other. Thus the equality and dignity of all human beings lies at the basis of our morality.

What we perhaps can agree on is that some actions are more effective in making our societies functional than others. We then can have a meaningful conversation about what those actions might be among those of all faiths. We can maintain the view that we all are worthwhile human beings while clarifying the goals that will best serve humanity and determining how to reach them. We hopefully can learn from those who hold beliefs that are different from our own and gain a larger perspective on what might be true.

The essential vision behind every religion is the divine origin of the creation and thus every thing and person that is a part of it. People who see this as the message of their religion will represent that view in their interactions. Violent acts in the name of a religion or a religious figure – no matter how justified they seem at the time – are acts against the creation and the creator. With this in mind, we can become a model for constructive communication between those of different beliefs.

Those who adhere to religion hope for it to provide answers to our quest for meaning. When the ancient Greeks traveled to Delphi for an answer to their major life questions they were given only general admonitions that forced seekers to look within themselves. For those who pursue answers in the pages of the Bible, Koran, or other holy texts, confirmation of our connection to the divine can be found. Members of Eastern religions understand that personal transformation is the result of contemplating the wisdom within. Meaning ultimately is experienced by each of us as we connect with a force both beyond and within ourselves.

Religious practice that reflects the larger truth of the value of every person is that which is most in touch with the force that put us here and most likely to sustain us for the future. As I once heard a pastor say at an Oakland church, "Real worship leads to service."

By respecting and honoring the divine in every human being we also respect our creator, whether that be a divine being or a primordial force. For those who are religious and those who are not, we can move toward fulfillment of the intent of that force by showing respect for the persons and entities that make up our world.

9. Justice

KEY PRINCIPLE: *In democracies justice is based on the principle that everyone is to be treated equally in the eyes of the law.*

In our distant past when we formed tribes, it increased our chance of survival by allowing us to work together toward common goals. Sublimating one's aggressiveness for the cohesion of the whole was expected.[135] For the survival of a group – or nation – a system of justice is essential to curbing antisocial behavior. Because of our tribal instincts we might see those outside our group not being as worthy as ourselves, or not even human at all, which can be a basis for persecution or war.

The traditional symbol of justice is a balanced scale, often held in one hand by a blindfolded woman with a sword in her other hand to represent swiftness. The Egyptians, Greeks, and Romans all had a similar image which has been brought forward to the democracies of our time. Its meaning is that equal justice is an essential ingredient of civilization. But in the myths of those ancient cultures the gods always played favorites.

In our Western tradition the idea of justice has roots in the concept of one God who treats everyone equally.

This can be found in the Torah, which later became part of the Old Testament. As the Israelites meandered through the desert, Moses dealt with the daunting task of "judging the people" which was beyond the ability of any one person. His father-in-law Jethro suggested that judges be trained to handle disputes.

Choose good men you can trust – men who respect God. Choose men who will not change their decisions for money. Make these men rulers over the people. There should be rulers over 1000 people, 100 people, 50 people, and even over ten people…If there is a very important case, they can come to you and let you decide what to do. But they can decide the other cases themselves. In this way these men will share your work, and it will be easier for you to lead the people.[136]

Their judicial system depended on the individual judgments of men. It did not provide the laws needed for people to govern themselves. Soon afterwards God revealed those laws to Moses in the form of the Ten Commandments.[137] Thus we have a model for a legal system based on a written rule of law rather than decrees of individuals.

In democracies justice is based on the principle of everyone being equal before the law. We have progressed in that direction, although along the way our laws – and courts – have allowed slavery, segregation, unequal treatment of women and persecution of minorities. From the perspective of the future our current understanding of human equality also may look naïve.

John Locke was one of the English "Enlightenment" writers whose works inspired the American rebellion against the crown. Locke argued against the doctrine of "divine right of kings" in the early 1700s.

God gave no immediate power to Adam over men....
God gave him right in common with all Mankind; so neither
was he Monarch.[138]

That is to say that there is no inherent right of kings
to govern others, and that all men are equally valuable
in God's eyes. This was a radical concept for its time.

Thomas Paine, writing in support of the American
Revolution in 1776, inspired many with his incendiary
words.

The cause of America is, in a great measure, the cause
of all mankind.[139]

His idea was that a sense of justice is latent in the
human soul until circumstances allow it to emerge.

The US Constitution, ratified in 1789, declared a
standard for human rights that was the most progressive for its day. It begins with a phrase affirming that
the people are the source of all power in government.

We the People of the United States, in Order to form
a more perfect Union, establish Justice, insure domestic
Tranquility, provide for the common defence, promote the
general Welfare, and secure the Blessings of Liberty to
ourselves and our Posterity, do ordain and establish this
Constitution for the United States of America.

But the idea of human equality inherent in the
phrase "We the People" – despite considerable progress – still is evolving. Stating democratic principles,
while innovative, is not nearly the same as living
them. Bringing these principles into everyday practice
requires not just new laws, but new norms in human
interaction.[140] This has been an ongoing struggle as we
slowly have affirmed the rights of those who were left
out at the founding.

One of the early US Supreme Court Justices, John Marshall, established that leaders must be subordinate to the Constitution, and that it is the role of the courts to determine the meaning of laws.

It is emphatically the provenance and duty of the judiciary department to say what the law is...the Constitution is superior to any ordinary act of the legislature; the Constitution, and not an ordinary act, must govern the case to which they both apply.[141]

He also emphasized that the Constitution is a living document, written so that its meaning would evolve with changing times.

[The Constitution is] intended to ensure for the ages... for exigencies which, if foreseen at all, must have been seen dimly, and which can best be provided for as they occur.[142]

An essential principle in democracies is equal justice and fairness for all. We generally have moved closer to this goal as we continue to discover the meaning of human equality promised in the constitutions of all nations, even those not considered democratic.[143]

In *A Theory of Justice*, perhaps the most esteemed work on the subject, John Rawls states his Two Principles of Justice.

First: each person is to have an equal right to the most extensive basic liberty compatible with similar liberty for others.

Second: social and economic inequalities are to be arranged so that they are both (a) reasonably expected to be to everyone's advantage, and (b) attached to positions and offices open to all.[144]

The main emphasis in Rawls is that there only is justice in a society when it is equally applied to each of us. The liberty of everyone is intertwined. In democracies the role of government is to ensure equal treatment in all areas in which it functions.

Throughout the evolution of democracies we have expanded our idea of those to whom equal rights should be extended. A partial list includes Native Americans, blacks, Hispanics, women, and sexual minorities, but as rights are affirmed for those previously denied we discover new groups to whose rights we once were blind. The process continues to evolve with our expanding definition of human liberty.

To that end, democratic leadership welcomes diverse viewpoints in pursuit of truth. But as they forged a new nation, the US founders demonstrated that divergent views ultimately must meld into consensus to create a viable nation. George Washington warned against extreme partisanship that would blind us to the purpose of the hard fought American Revolution, which was to secure liberty for everyone.

The common and continual mischiefs of the spirit of party are sufficient to make it the interest and duty of a wise people to discourage and restrain it.[145]

If, in democracies, everyone is to receive equal justice, then we must move beyond a view that the interests of some are superior to others and work together toward the perspective – expressed in our actions as well as our laws – that all people deserve to have their rights given equal consideration. To make justice a lived reality, we each must apply its most basic principle of respect for every human being, not just as an ideal, but in every aspect of our governments and lives.

John Finnis, in his classic **Natural Law and Natural**

Rights, emphasizes what he considers the three elements of justice.

*1) Other-directedness: Justice has to do with one's rela-
tions and dealings with other persons.*

*2) Duty: What is owed to another and...what that per-
son has a right to.*

*3) Equality: Think of proportionality, or even of equilib-
rium or balance between people.*[146]

When I treat others fairly I affirm my belief in a
just society. Justice is not something that is achieved
solely by laws because people can twist laws to their
own advantage. Justice only is achieved by individuals interacting with each other in a way that acknowl-
edges their rights and human dignity while affirming
their own.

10. International Relations

KEY PRINCIPLE: *Democracies support the ideal of human dignity both domestically and internationally.*

Tribalism once helped humans survive because it provided an edge in hunting, mating, and war. As tribes expanded into states and nations they enhanced their survival chances by enlarging their pool of natural and human resources. Cooperation toward common goals with those beyond the tribe enabled our ancestors to create civilizations.

But the divisiveness of tribalism remains in our genes. We often focus on the negative in others, especially for members of groups that we see as different than our own. In our minds this can be enough to justify a verbal or physical attack. We must be prepared to defend ourselves, but putting a mental wall between us and others increases enmity and the likelihood that aggression will take place.

The First World War showed us the consequences of stumbling into aggression with little forethought.[147] After that war, resentment festered due to punishments imposed on Germany by the victors, which led to the even larger conflagration of World War II.[148]

Between these wars – although drawn into both late in the game – the US tried a return to isolationism. But that proved impossible as the Second World War encompassed Europe and the Japanese attacked Pearl Harbor on December 7, 1941.

After the huge human and economic losses that resulted from that war, democracies seemed to at last have learned the lessons of the danger of isolationism. Before its end, 44 nations, weary of conflict, established a system to provide economic support for winners and losers alike at a conference in Bretton Woods, New Hampshire.[149] Then after the war ended in 1945, 50 countries established the United Nations to deal cooperatively with international issues. The US and its partners formed organizations to support trade and provide a united front against the growing threat of totalitarianism. These included GATT (General Agreement on Tariffs and Trades, now the World Trade Organization) and NATO (North Atlantic Treaty Organization.)

We had learned in the West, at least for a while, the need to look past nationality and ethnicity to work together for mutual benefit. During the thirty plus years after World War II – despite some down economic periods – the general trend was toward greater prosperity. This was the period described by the French as *les trente glorieuses*, the Germans as *Wirtschaft swunder*, and the Italians as *miracolo economico*.[150]

In that period the United States, which financed much of the recovery, was seen across the free world as an example of a well-functioning democracy that, while far from perfect, was moving with other democracies steadily in the direction of increased prosperity. The US sponsored the rebuilding of many countries through programs such as the Marshall Plan that benefitted their allies and former enemies.[151]

But toward the latter part of that period the moral authority of the US and other democracies began to fade. A younger generation challenged leaders in many countries that, as they saw it, abandoned essential democratic principles. To them the world seemed caught in materialism while ignoring the ideal of human equality they had been taught. Democracies were waging wars against small countries like Vietnam and propping up dictators.[152]

Economic growth also seemed to slow down for many, and there was malaise among those who found themselves caught in what they considered meaningless work and lives. Protests by youth and workers broke out in the late 1960s, angering members of the generation that had built the post-war economy. Discontent exploded in strikes and riots in the US, France, Hong Kong, and other places.[153] Alternative dress and lifestyles were adopted by young people who sought to create an identity separate from what they considered the soulless lifestyle of their parents' generation.

By the end of the 1970s an alarmed electorate reacted by putting more conservative leaders in place. Margaret Thatcher became British Prime Minister in 1979 followed by Ronald Reagan as US President in 1981. Thatcher famously said: "I'm not a consensus politician," and ultimately was ousted for her refusal to back an expanding role for Britain in the European community.[154] Reagan took an aggressive stance toward those who would dare challenge him, including anyone who would protest or strike, or those he considered unproductive members of society.[155] The lesson of the importance of international cooperation seemed to fade for Britain and the US, which adopted a "go it alone" attitude while maintaining only a tenuous relationship with international bodies like the UN, except to seek support in its confrontation with Communist nations.[156]

For much of history the United States was considered a "city on a hill" to people and countries aspiring to democracy. US Presidents brought together world leaders to negotiate peace agreements such as the Camp David summit between Israel and the Palestinians by Jimmy Carter in 1978,[157] and meetings to end hostilities in Northern Ireland by Bill Clinton in 1998.[158] But in its desire for stable partners, the US also supported oppressive leaders such as Batista in Cuba and the Shah (Emperor) of Iran.[159] In these places and others, when rebels overthrew autocrats in the hope of greater freedom, they enabled new despots to come into power.

As the major democracies turned away from their leadership role the world became less stable. The international cooperation that sprang up in the wake of World War II began to fade. Reagan's famous demand to the Soviets to tear down the Berlin Wall was not matched by a pro-active stance to work with the UN to support struggling nations. The view that international financial stability and that of the individual were intertwined yielded to a view that every nation – and person – now was on its own.[160]

In this century there have been countries that

seemed to be moving in the direction of democracy, but instead have backtracked toward authoritarianism, including Venezuela, Russia, Poland and Hungary.[161] In Venezuela, after Hugo Chavez came into office he changed the country's constitution to allow him to assume absolute power.[162] In Russia, Vladimir Putin was legitimately elected but soon dismantled that country's fledgling democratic institutions.[163] In Poland, the so-called Law and Justice party eliminated press freedom and subverted the country's constitution to consolidate power.[164] In Hungary, Victor Orban stated that democracy "should be hierarchical rather than liberal."[165]

In nations that still consider themselves democracies, despite what some politicians and economists claim is steady economic growth, many people are losing faith in their future.[166] They are economically stagnating and they support strong leaders who blame others for their country's problems based on race, religion, or political affiliation. Some want clear and simple answers to dilemmas such as immigration, which they believe – incorrectly – to be threatening their jobs.[167] Many have an unfavorable view of democracy because they believe it fails to support their needs.[168]

Because of growing economic disparity in these nations, the chorus of discontent is getting louder.[169] The expansion of what many call "populism" is the response.[170] As much of the world slips toward autocracy, the principle of human equality – the founding ideal of democracy – is not discussed by their leaders. They promise security but never mention human dignity or freedom. Security is to be found, they claim, by identifying those who are to blame. They never clearly mention the consequences likely to come out of those views. Are we to marginalize or even eliminate those we blame for our country's problems?

The appeal of these leaders is strongest to those who have forgotten the ethnic hatred that led to the great conflicts of the last century. They have failed to improve the lot of those who see themselves as struggling and have moved the world further from democracy as they tighten their grip.

For democracy to survive we need to identify a way forward to restore the rights and livelihoods of those who believe themselves left behind. What, if anything, can be done to restore the economic balance that we saw in the post-war period?

The thrust of Western democracies largely has shifted from working together to lift each other up, to pursuing their needs without regard for others or the world community. Our trade agreements once were designed to protect nations and their inhabitants, but they slowly have shifted to serve mainly those with financial and political clout.[171] The result has been a world largely wrought in inequality.

Western democracies have been unwilling to put pressure on countries like Poland and Hungary where the rights of those not politically connected are under siege. In these places a new elite is being established that deprives those who are targeted of rights and economic opportunity.[172]

Countries who want to see democracy maintained must make a clear stand that violations of human rights will not be tolerated. The positive side of this approach can be returning to a Marshall Plan framework to help struggling countries move toward a more prosperous economy. Democracies can encourage training and rebuilding to put structures into place – roads, bridges, schools, health systems – that create jobs and a sense of pride. We can return to the view that the problems of all nations are intertwined; that we have a need and responsibility to work across fences and borders to stabilize our world. Economic incentives can encourage reluctant countries – and their regimes – to emerge from their descent into autocracy.

If positive incentives don't work, then democratic nations can exert economic pressure to encourage these countries to re-commit themselves to human rights. Measures can include sanctions, refusal to engage in trade, and international isolation. But perhaps the most effective way to exert pressure is to lead by example; to show that democracies can provide training and jobs in the green economy, and that they are willing to offer a hand to nations who aspire to do this until they are standing on their own feet. This, in turn, will bring greater stability everywhere.

Actions by democracies are more effective – and seen as more just – when done in cooperation with other nations, but US often has opted to act alone. The first Iraq war, in 1991, was in response to an invasion of Kuwait that involved a coalition of 35 nations. During the second Iraq war, in 2003, the US attacked based on manufactured information and only was joined by Britain. At other times, the US has failed to keep its promises which resulted in increased suffering. In 2013, Barack Obama promised to punish the regime in Syria if it used chemical weapons on its rebels but he never followed through.[173] In 2019 Donald Trump abandoned the Kurds who had been US partners in fighting Syria. These failures resulted in condemnation by world leaders and both American political parties.[174]

Poland is a prime example of a country that has fallen short of its democratic aspirations. That country has had changing borders due to numerous invasions and partitions going back to at least 1717, when it came under the rule of Russia.[175] In 1791, Poland was the earliest Eastern European country to establish a constitution guaranteeing democracy, but that effort was overthrown the very next year by Russia.[176]

Poland also has a history of following autocrats and willing participation in the persecution of minorities. It provides an example of what can happen when those who have been persecuted revert to a tribalism that takes over the hearts and minds of those who no longer consider the "other" as human. My grandparents immigrated to the US about 1900 when they fled pogroms, or persecutions, that swept through Poland and other Eastern European countries in waves.[177] But Poland also was one of the first countries to break from the Soviet bloc in 1989 and establish a democracy. After it bolted from Soviet grip, democracy received a bad name because oligarchs helped themselves to what had been state resources. This also happened in Russia.

Poland – like all countries – has had individuals who treat minorities with respect and those who persecute them. Before and during World War II there were many examples of Poles who hid Jews and those who willingly participated in exterminating Jews.[178] True democracies always are willing to admit and correct their failures to prevent them from reoccurring. But in a departure from history and from the transparency essential to real democracy, the President of Poland, Andrzej Duda, signed a bill in 2018 threatening three years in prison for anyone who "publicly and untruthfully assigns responsibility to the Polish nation or Polish state for Nazi crimes."[179]

There are two contradictory historical elements reflected in the Polish psyche – a long-standing desire for independence and a wish for retribution toward anyone who can be blamed for their country's ills. Currently Poland has a government that rewards those who support its autocracy at the expense of those who do not. Its populist regime is eroding the rule of law except for those who participate in its oppression.[180]

How do we encourage countries with failing democracies to steer back to the path of equality and human rights? In reality, it is people who deal with each other, not nations. Countries – like people – are unlikely ever to "behave." Just like the people who occupy them, their composition is complex – their mood is at times angry, gentle, judgmental or kind – as are their leaders. Despite human nature, or because of it, clear standards need to be established among democracies for what is permissible and what is not – within their own nations and others – based on the principles of human dignity and equal rights. Enforcement must be applied as consistently and unwaveringly as possible.[181] A continued diminishment of democracy around the world is likely unless those in countries who believe in it reignite its beacon and do what is needed to restore human rights.

International relations only are personal relations on a larger scale. We all have our shortcomings. So – just as with people – it is with humility we must approach other nations that we see as falling outside the realm of respect for human rights. Then, in concert with other democracies, we must do everything we can – short of war – to insist that human dignity around the world be held sacred.

The search for truth strains the patience of most people, who would rather believe the first thing that comes to mind.

— Thucydides, ***History of The Peloponnesian War*** (1.20.3)

Summary and Possible Lessons

The word democracy is from the ancient Greek, meaning "government by the people." The US Constitution states that "We the People" are both the creators and beneficiaries of democracy.

When those who see themselves as being under tyranny decide to rebel, they create a plan to organize their insurrection. Once freedom is won, the new leaders begin the even more difficult task of generating a government to retain their hard fought liberties.

Rebellions don't always result in democracy. In the US – due to the vision of its founders and its Constitution – the promise of equal rights slowly has expanded to a larger segment of the population, including women and minorities. But the fulfillment of that promise still is far from complete in the US and most other democracies.

A key issue is how to maintain individual freedoms while keeping a strong government in place. This requires visionary and committed leadership that can draw lessons from the past to move us boldly into the future while being guided by the principle of human equality. Effective leaders rely on the best talents available as they work together toward solutions to the issues of their day. No leader is without flaws, but some are not up to the challenging task of balancing the rights of all the people.

In democracies we make decisions about how to act – as individuals, groups and governments – based on the principle of human equality and the best information available. Despite our best-laid plans, unexpected events can at any time blow us off course. We then must expand our idea of what works best to include new information and enable us to once again move forward.

Democracies at times are confronted with new truths that threaten their existence and they need to respond. This only can be done effectively in partnership with other nations. Despite the difficulties in coming to consensus, no nation can defeat the scourges that face us without working with as many partners as possible to prepare for what happens next.

In the wake of the 2001 attacks on the World Trade Center and Pentagon in the US, and similar attacks in other nations, a new understanding of the serious threats that face us emerged. Add to this catastrophes that strike without regard to national or ethnic boundaries, including natural disasters such as our current world-wide pandemic. Each of these teaches us – if we are open to the lesson – that the world we thought we knew no longer exists.

Once – when we lived in small tribes – we took part in group decision making. As our social units enlarged to the level of states and nations, our leaders made the major decisions for our society. In exchange for giving them that power we were able to live in societies with greater stability and comfort. In most nations the accepted truth became that our rulers and their judgments are superior to those of everyone else. Inequality became the norm. Thomas Hobbes famously wrote that in our natural condition life is "solitary, poor, nasty, brutish, and short."[182] And so – he maintained – better any state than none.

Throughout history people have rebelled to replace rulers who didn't serve their interests. But some leaders did see the importance of addressing the needs of the people to stabilize their society. Thus in ancient Athens, democracy or "government by the people," was born with its commitment to "equal justice for all."[183]

The main principle of democracy is that all are created equal and entitled to be treated fairly. That idea slowly came into play in England starting with the Magna Carta of 1215. Human equality was one of the "self-evident" truths mentioned in the US Declaration of Independence, and then it was re-envisioned, with ways to make it a lived reality, by the US Constitution. Democracy eventually was attempted in over 100 nations. But it is much easier to state the truth of human equality than to bring it into practice in the real world.

Our idea of what is true affects our decisions at

all levels and evolves with time. For most of human history it was assumed that rulers and their decisions were superior to those of their subjects, but now the concept of human rights is written into every constitution, even in non-democratic countries.[184] Our model for what is true has been greatly expanded by those who have explored the world and by scientific advancement. This has moved us from a belief that the cosmos revolves around the earth to a realization that we are but a speck in a universe beyond our imagining.

Thanks to the progress of our knowledge we now know how to alter our environment to bring us longer and healthier lives. We have moved from living in the wild at the mercy of our surroundings to creating shelters that provide protection from the elements. We have mastered food production on a mass scale so that most of us only need to participate in the economy to procure our needs rather than scrounging our surroundings in hope of a successful hunt. Many of the scientific advances of the last 200 years – from the steam engine to life saving vaccines – have been nurtured in the bosom of democracies that emphasize the importance of human dignity.

But despite our comforts there still is much lacking in our understanding. There are threats brought by nature that are beyond what our science can prevent. Among these are earthquakes, floods, hurricanes, and epidemics. Some people have been left behind despite a booming economy.[185] For many, life is dominated by inner dissatisfaction despite what appears to be material success.[186]

And then there is a current crisis of leadership in our

democracies. People who believe they were left behind or have seen injustice in their countries have risen up to elect leaders they hope will correct that unfairness. But some leaders distort the truth and fix blame for their nation's problems rather than working with others to overcome them. They sow division as they fail to focus on the human equality and dignity that are the corner-stones of democracy. These "populist" leaders thrive on what they claim are the failure of others rather than building coalitions to address pressing issues. This movement that infects many democracies makes one wonder if it even is possible for a government to meet the needs of its people.

As I write this a coronavirus (COVID-19) pandemic encircles the globe. This is a new crisis for which no vaccine has been developed to date. The situation is overwhelming hospitals and decimating economies worldwide. Such a disease would be problematic in democracies working in coordination with each other to limit its effects, but what has allowed it to spread quickly and become more devastating is a lack of planning and transparency by many nations – some democratic and some not. Denying the true extent of this threat allowed it to spread quickly – initially in China – making it much more deadly than it would otherwise have been.[187] The Prime Minister of Britain contracted the virus with a number of associates after being in close contact in violation of recommendations of health authorities.[188] Following the best advice of scientists, who recommend extensive testing, social distancing, and isolating the most serious cases, has limited its effect in countries such as South Korea,[189]

Taiwan, New Zealand, Australia and Nigeria.[190]

The US had numerous warnings from health officials – many in the President's own political party – at least six weeks in advance of it becoming a domestic crisis, but that advice was ignored by a leader who favored political expediency over truth.[191] Now reality is forced upon the US by a crisis that threatens to overwhelm its healthcare system. There is no coordinated nationwide approach to precautionary procedures like closing non-essential businesses, social distancing or manufacturing and distributing essential protective equipment such as masks and respirators. The result has been an escalation of the danger and many needless deaths.[192] Because of the lack of a coordinated national effort, states had to compete between themselves and with the federal government in bidding for life-saving medical equipment. The US now has surpassed every other country in coronavirus cases and there will be thousands of deaths due to poor planning and coordination.

Maintaining preparations to provide contingency planning is an essential part of any government that hopes to learn from history and be ready for the inevitable emergency. The US has been woefully inadequate in this regard.[193]

The failure of leadership in much of the world in this health crisis – including Italy, Spain, Russia, Iran and the US – is an example of what can happen when leaders deny the truth until reality forces itself upon them. As they impose their ideology, truth fails to inform their views and actions.

In each of the ten major areas we have covered in this book – and in every other possible area – decisions need to be made based on the best information available rather than on a denial of science and wishful thinking that a serious problem will disappear. Leaders who support democracy are honest and transparent with their constituents. They rely on a confluence of experts to make the best decisions possible. Autocrats – or leaders with autocratic tendencies – make their decisions without transparency. Their allegiance is only to the part of the population they consider their allies.

We will summarize the areas discussed in previous chapters and then consider the type of leadership needed for democracy to succeed.

Interpersonal relations among individuals, groups and those in governments can be democratic or undemocratic. Democratic relationships are guided by the principles of human dignity and equality for everyone.

Politics and Government only function well when the vast majority of people believe that they are treated equally and with respect for their needs by the public servants who run their government.

Education that supports democracy teaches interpersonal communication and critical thinking in addition to technical skills. This prepares students to function effectively in a changing world.

Economics that is compatible with democracy helps to boost the lifestyles of those at every level of the economic scale to increase economic flow and security for all.

Science in democracies is focused on making discoveries that improve the lives of everyone.

The Environment connects people everywhere to the world around them. Thus our actions must reflect

121

an awareness that what we do to our environment is what we do to ourselves.

Health for anyone depends on health for everyone. Quality healthcare must therefore be universal.

Religion that is compatible with democracy teaches the value of all human beings.

Justice in democracy is equally applied to those of all economic levels and ethnic backgrounds.

International Relations are an extension of our personal relationships to people around the world. It is up to democratic nations to demand that the human rights of everyone are respected.

Leaders who affirm the truth of universal human equality move democracy forward. Leaders who deny that truth move democracy backwards. Since the US – for many – is considered the modern beacon of democracy we will review the records of the most consequential US presidents to see where they have affirmed or repudiated the principle of human equality. We do this not to assign blame, but to help determine where we have done well or poorly in our effort to absorb and apply what are the most significant lessons of history. This will allow us to move forward with clarity in the true spirit of human dignity upon which democracies are founded.

All American presidents have had good intentions yet, being human, all were flawed, as we all are. At the least, all care about their legacy. Yet we still can review their records regarding their commitment to upholding the principles that underlie democracy. The lessons for our day must be on what we can learn to ensure democratic values and practices for ourselves and future generations.

In "10 Lessons from History About What Makes a Great Leader," Andrew Roberts, author of *Leadership in War*, asks: "What are the qualities that a truly great American president needs?" He breaks it down to nine essential characteristics: energy, an ability to plan and adapt to changing circumstances, a great memory, understanding public sentiment, well-timed unreasonableness, steady nerves, inspiring persistence, empathy, and political awareness. All of these are part of an ability to respond to an ever-changing reality based on the principle of human equality. We will review the records of the following US presidents with that in mind.

George Washington (1789-97)

Washington rose from a mediocre general fighting on the side of the British in the Indian wars to a visionary leader without whom there likely would be no United States. He resigned after two terms as President to make a clear statement that no man should be king. In his *Farewell Address* he admonished the young nation to maintain its allegiance to the principles of democracy and avoid becoming more loyal to individuals or parties than to the country's core values. Among his flaws were a quick temper and maintaining slaves.

John Adams (1797-1801)

The second US President was a radical visionary who signed the US *Declaration of Independence*. He was a Northerner who opposed slavery and was the candidate of the Federalist Party in opposition to the Democratic-Republican Party of Jefferson. Adams named John Marshall as the fourth Chief Justice of the United States, who became a great champion of equal justice and who played a significant role in the development of the American legal system. Adams was known for his volatile temper and unwillingness to compromise, as well as his long feud with his one-time friend Jefferson who defeated him for the presidency.[194]

Thomas Jefferson (1801-1809)

The third US President was a Virginia gentleman who crafted the *Declaration of Independence* in a compromise that took weeks to complete. He forged the phrase – and was committed to the concept – that "all men are created equal." The slave trade was outlawed under his administration, but his vision of equality, though radical for the time, left out women and his own slaves.

James Madison (1809-1817)

Madison was a US founder who tempered his idealism with a realistic view of human nature. An author of the US Constitution, he was concerned that "passion never fails to wrest the scepter from reason." He worked to include the Bill of Rights although originally he opposed it.[195] His declaration of war against Britain in 1812 almost cost the US its independence as the British overran the US capital, only to be defeated at the Battle of New Orleans by Andrew Jackson. Madison also was a slave holder.

James Monroe (1817-1825)

The Monroe Doctrine (1823) closed the New World to further European colonization. It established the US as a kindly umbrella shielding the budding independent nations of Latin America from European interference and clarified that the desire of Russia to colonize further south on the Pacific coast would not be tolerated.[196] While railing against slavery, he took his slaves with him to the White House.

Andrew Jackson (1829-1837)

A brilliant general who defeated the British at the Battle of New Orleans (1815), Jackson was impulsive and almost court-marshaled for exceeding his mandate when he marched into Florida to confront Spanish forces.[197] He was perhaps the first "populist" leader who railed against established moneyed interests. He also was an Indian hater who defied the John Marshall Supreme Court by ordering the forced evacuation of Cherokees from Georgia and North Carolina to Oklahoma in winter on the "trail of tears" in which half of those marching – about 15,000 – died.

Abraham Lincoln (1861-1865)

Considered by many the greatest US president, Lincoln's shortened time in office was perhaps the most consequential. He was the first president of the newly formed anti-slavery Republican Party. He was a man of great compassion who, nonetheless, acted decisively when the Confederacy attacked Union troops at Fort Sumter, and changed generals who he thought were too indecisive. He assembled his cabinet from a "team of rivals"[198] so that he could be exposed to as many views as possible to aid him in making crucial decisions. He also displayed great magnanimity in refusing to punish the South after the Civil War, yet still believed in acting firmly on the truth as he saw it: "With malice toward none, with charity for all, with firmness in the right as God gives us to see the right."[199] Yet he violated the Constitution when he suspended the right of habeas corpus (holding prisoners without charging them) to prevent a possible attack on Washington D.C. He had frequent bouts of depression and fretted that he would not have enough troops to conduct the war.[200]

Theodore Roosevelt (1901-1909)

"Speak softly and carry a big stick" is probably his most famous quote, and it aptly summarized his approach to foreign policy, although he probably ventured more on the "stick" side of the equation. A sickly child who greatly improved his stamina by determination and exercise, he was an ardent conservationist and opponent of the monopolies that dominated the lives of most Americans. But he also was an imperialist who participated in the Spanish American War and wrote unabashedly on white superiority, exemplified by a speech he gave in 1909 in which he stated that those under imperialism should be grateful for cultural benefits brought them by "The Expansion of the White Races"[201]

Woodrow Wilson (1913-1921)

A Harvard intellectual and visionary who saw the threat of World War I encroaching on the US but who failed to act until after the sinking of the passenger liner Lusitania in 1915.[202] He established the Federal Reserve System and won the Nobel Peace Prize for his contribution to founding the League of Nations after the war. He also established the Federal Trade Commission to regulate questionable business practices and promoted the Smith–Lever Act which helped farmers learn new agricultural techniques as well as the Federal Farm Loan Act to increase credit to rural family farmers. The Adamson Act established an eight-hour workday, with overtime pay, for interstate railroad workers. He signed the 19th Amendment to the U.S. Constitution in 1920 which prohibits any citizen from being denied the right to vote on the basis of sex. On the other hand, he was an extreme racist, which affected his policies.[203]

Herbert Hoover (1929-1933)

Much-maligned for inaction during the Great Depression that started in 1930, Hoover's statements showed that he was out of touch with reality until the worst hit: "Business and industry have turned the corner" (January 21, 1930), and "We have now passed the worst" (May 1, 1930). Protectionist tariffs like the Hawley-Smoot Act of 1930 made things worse by weakening economic flow. His laissez-faire views and inability to accurately assess the situation allowed things to deteriorate further. Unemployment peaked at 25% in 1931. Eventually Hoover did make efforts to curtail the disaster with measures like the Reconstruction Finance Corporation of 1932 created for loaning to large businesses, but he was unwilling to put direct relief into place. His meager efforts turned out to be ineffective as the situation imploded.[204]

Franklin Roosevelt (1933-1945)

Coming into office toward the beginning of the Great Depression, Roosevelt at first blundered by trying to cut federal spending. The Emergency Banking Relief Act, initiated right after his inauguration, guaranteed that at least some banks would stay open and encouraged people to reopen accounts. The New Deal, a cornucopia of relief measures, included unemployment assistance, help for farmers, infrastructure rebuilding, and limiting bank speculation.[205] After the Supreme Court blocked some of his initiatives, Roosevelt tried to pack the Court by adding judges, but this idea was rejected by both Democrats and Republicans.[206] His economic programs, however, did not pull the nation out of the Depression until the massive spending of World War II circulated money to all levels of the economy. His fireside chats, where he invited Americans into his "living room," and his stirring speeches with memorable phrases like "We have nothing to fear but fear itself," inspired the American people at a time when they most needed it. His shortcomings were numerous, such as his decision to inter Japanese Americans based on no evidence of collaboration, and his refusal to consider admitting Jews fleeing Nazi persecution. He also had a number of liaisons with women outside of his marriage.

Harry Truman (1945-1953)

Truman took over on Roosevelt's death in April 1945 and was responsible for the decision to drop two atom bombs on Japan after its refusal to surrender. He continued the policies of rebuilding the US and supporting countries after World War II – friend and foe alike – via the Marshall Plan and other programs. At the end of the war he and Churchill confronted Stalin at the 1945 Potsdam conference in an effort to win the right to vote for Eastern European countries, but could make little headway because the Soviets already had most of that territory in its grip.[207] Truman recognized Israel and initiated the Berlin Airlift in 1948. He dealt with the Korean War after South Korea was attacked from the North in 1950, and then moved decisively – but with counsel from his advisors – to remove General Douglass MacArthur from his post after he violated policy and spoke out as a decision-maker. He gave an order to integrate the armed services in the same year. He confronted McCarthyism in the 1950s amidst unfounded accusations of communist influence in the Democratic Party. He nearly always stuck to his principles, although at times he was described as being stubborn.

Dwight Eisenhower (1953-1961)

I still recall "I Like Ike" posters on homes throughout my neighborhood in my youth. What made him likeable, in addition to being the general who commanded Allied forces in the war, was a steady and easy-going personality. But despite his decisiveness as Supreme Allied Commander, Eisenhower, who had no previous political experience, often was indecisive as President as he relegated decisions about crises during his administration to his subordinates, including John Foster Dulles, his Secretary of State.[208] Under his administration the US overthrew elected governments in Iran and Guatemala suspected of leaning too far left.[209] His enforcement of civil rights was limited. He regretted appointing Earl Warren as Supreme Court Justice when, as a result of the 1954 "Brown vs. Board of Education" decision, Eisenhower was forced to bring in federal troops to maintain order in Little Rock, Arkansas.[210] But through what he called "Dynamic Conservatism" he enlarged Social Security, raised the minimum wage, and launched a nationwide highway program.

John Kennedy (1961-1963)

Many people to this day remember where they were when Kennedy was shot. The vanguard of a new generation of youthful leadership, he would be over 100 if alive today. His clarity of purpose and decisiveness sometimes worked well and sometimes revealed a lack of consideration of all the possible consequences of his actions. In an escalation of US efforts to avoid what was feared to be a gradual communist takeover of Asia, he increased the presence of military "advisors" in Vietnam from 685 to over 16,000.[211] The 1961 Bay of Pigs invasion to remove Fidel Castro from Cuba was a failure, but his masterful confrontation the next year of the Soviet buildup of missiles in Cuba provided much relief for a world that feared nuclear war might end it all. He included men of both parties in his cabinet and listened to their views before making his own decisions. He personified a belief in human dignity as made clear in a June, 1963 speech where he declared "no government or social system is so evil that its people must be considered as lacking in virtue." But his affairs with women attracted to his youth and vigor have put a stain on his legacy.

Lyndon Johnson (1963-1969)

Johnson was able to succeed in getting civil rights legislation passed that Congress had blocked under Kennedy, partly because of a unity of purpose in the trail of Kennedy's death and partly because of Johnson's mastery of the legislative process that he developed as a senator. He was the champion of a Great Society that included his "war on poverty,"[212] but denied the ugly truth of the buildup of casualties in Vietnam that eventually forced him out of office.[213] Under his leadership, important programs that now seem essential were passed, such as the Civil Rights Act of 1964, the Clean Air Act, the Department of Housing and Urban Development, the Fair Housing Act, the Fair Immigration Law, the Farm Program, Food Stamps, Medicare, Pesticide Controls, and the Voting Rights Act.[214]

Richard Nixon (1969-1974)

Known primarily for being the only president to resign and for his paranoid, vindictive personality, Nixon's accomplishments often are overlooked. He inherited the "domino theory" of his two predecessors which showed in his stubborn pursuit of the Vietnam War from which he led a hasty exit in 1973. But during his term he also established trade with China, which would have been politically impossible for a Democrat, and signed into law the Environmental Protection Agency which subsequent Republicans would try to eviscerate. He did drag the moral image of the US Presidency to a new low by ordering the break-in at the DC Democratic Headquarters, which only was exposed when Nixon was forced by the courts to release the covert recordings of his White House conversations relating to the break-in.

Jimmy Carter (1977-1981)

You may not think of Jimmy Carter as a consequential president, but he set an example by his morality and effectiveness after leaving office. His administration was beset by problems that may or may not have been of his doing, such as the hostage crisis in Iran and rampant inflation that began the unraveling of the 30 year post-war prosperity. He did not take a firm stance to combat those issues. His charitable character was perhaps best represented in the Habitat for Humanity housing organization to which he has devoted his post-presidential life. He exemplifies a lived Christianity that is an example for all. His motto was: "I will never lie to you," one that he actually lives up to according to historians.[215]

Ronald Reagan (1981-1989)

Reagan inspired a new populist movement that affected people of many political stripes threatened by the runaway inflation of the 1970s and concerned about America's role as the leading democracy by incidents such as the Iran hostage crisis. Reagan championed nuclear arms containment at the 1986 Reykjavik Summit, where he failed to secure a deal, but his pressure on the Soviet Union did result in serious dialogue. Some credit him with ending the Cold War with his famous speech: "Mr. Gorbachev, tear down this wall," but he also said that the Soviet Union would collapse of its own weight, which is closer to what happened. Reagan discussed freedom and human rights as he supported authoritarian governments in Central American and apartheid in South Africa.[216] His emphasis was on the idea that "government is the problem," rather than actually trying to make it work. Reagan drove a wedge between his followers and those they blamed, including those he considered welfare cheats (of which there actually were few) and air traffic controllers, who were fired in 1981 when they dared go on strike. He ended the post-war era of common purpose, when people were proud to pay taxes to support their country, and initiated an era when internal division replaced the idea of working together. Taxes were cut and the deficit soared, making the US a debtor nation for the first time.[217] The result of the Reagan years was a greater division among Americans and a deficit balloon that led to a recession for which his successor, George H. W. Bush, received the blame as he failed to win reelection in 1992.

Bill Clinton (1993-2001)

Clinton was the first president born of a generation that had not been alive at the time of the Second World War. He exuded a youthful confidence that permeated both his successes and failures. He followed through on his campaign promise to raise taxes and the economy recovered while the national debt shrank. In the international realm, Clinton inherited a number of difficult situations that he did not always handle competently – he regretted not intervening decisively in the Rwandan civil war in which 800,000 minority Tutsis were killed.[218] His support for the North American Free Trade Area legislation helped businesses reduce labor costs while sending jobs abroad. He worked with the International Monetary Fund through his Treasury

Secretary Robert Rubin to intervene in serious financial crises in Japan and Mexico. He hosted an Israeli-Palestinian peace conference in 2000 that seemed to hold out hope for real progress.[219] In 1999 he signed a bill that eliminated the requirement that banks separate their banking and investment functions, which ultimately led to the wild speculation of the Great Recession. His presidency was seriously marred by missteps including his affairs about which he lied, resulting in impeachment, and denying the harmful effects of his attempts to "end welfare as we know it."

George W. Bush (2001-2009)

Bush was awarded the presidency by a conservative Supreme Court after losing the national popular vote to Al Gore. He aggressively cut taxes for wealthy Americans that he claimed – as did Reagan before him and Trump afterwards – would boost the economy for everyone, but which instead increased the economic divide.[220] After the 2001 attacks he proved an inspiring leader for a while, going out of his way to visit Washington D.C mosques to assure Americans that the enemy is not the Muslim religion but those who use religion to justify hate. In 2003 he used falsified information to convince the US Congress to approve a war against Iraq without UN consensus, under the pretense that Saddam Hussein held "weapons of mass destruction" that never were found. That war lasted nine years. It cost thousands of lives and trillions of dollars.[221] It was used as an excuse for the morally questionable torture of the "enemy," as well as to justify domestic spying that was coordinated under Vice

President Dick Cheney.[222] Under Bush the world economy in 2008 entered the worst downturn since the Great Depression, largely as a result of reckless real estate speculation fueled by excess funds made available by tax cuts for the wealthy and interest rates that were kept artificially low. The stock market halved and Bush was disinvited from the 2008 Republican convention. His Troubled Asset Relief Program (TARP) pumped $700 billion into the economy and mostly helped banks stay afloat. But also under Bush, billions of dollars in funding for AIDS relief to Africa was provided. One more positive item, rarely noted, was the unprecedented diversity of his cabinet, which perhaps was instrumental in seeding the path for the next president.

Barack Obama (2009-2017)

It was a long time coming: the election of the first US president of African American heritage. He inherited an economy that threatened to descend into depression, two ongoing wars and the threat of a still strong Al Queda terrorist group. His financial rescue program – in addition to the TARP program of Bush – began a slow easing of the economy toward recovery by support of low income workers and the unemployed, rebuilding the country's infrastructure, helping to pay health care costs, supporting education and energy efficiency programs, and improving homeland security.[223] It also spurred the beginning of the "Tea Party" movement that objected to the government "paying people's mortgages," as Rick Santelli ranted on the NY stock exchange trading floor. Assuming he owned stocks, Rick Santelli benefitted enormously from the greatly improved economy that Obama rescued from Bush.

Obama was (and is) an incredibly intelligent and genial person: a remarkable wordsmith in both writing and speech who announced himself to the world in a speech to the 2004 Democratic Convention and two best-selling books. But he dropped one of his major ideas that he proposed to save the economy even before taking office: he had promised to raise taxes on everyone making over $250,000 per year – similar to what had worked under Bill Clinton – but discarded that idea. He also compromised a number of his ideas that he had eloquently championed. This greatly diluted his effectiveness and likely his legacy. His signature legislation – the Affordable Care Act – was delegated to his representatives in Congress and rarely pitched from the White House, which might have strengthened its support by the American people. He proposed to strike Syria if its leader used poison gas on his own people, but never followed through, a failure that even was criticized by Hillary Clinton. Osama bin Laden, the mastermind of the 2001 Trade Center attacks, was apprehended during his administration. A record number of immigrants were deported under his watch. His lack of decisiveness in supporting reforms that affected blacks – for example in the criminal justice system – earned the ire of black leaders.[224] But his kindly and caring demeanor, in addition to the ACA and regulations to curb pollution, are likely what he will most be remembered for.

Donald Trump (2017-   )

The most recent leaders loom the largest, and the current president looms largest of all because of his impact on our world and lives. If we are going to hold our present-day leaders to the same standards as those of the past we need to take a balanced view of their accomplishments and failures as best we can, with an eye on the leader's underlying views and leadership style.

People of all political persuasions would agree that Donald Trump brings a unique style to the American presidency. Most important is whether the leadership style of a president is suited to democracy. When we consider the essential standard of democracy – respect for human equality – how does this president hold up?

First, the good. Trump has united many people and given hope to some who thought that their lives – and needs – had been forgotten. Many people in the US and other countries – such as Britain – never have recovered from the Great Recession of 2008. The world economy as a whole came back from that cliff, but there are large pockets left behind, especially in areas where many lost their jobs – and often their homes – to the double punch of closing factories and economic downturn.

Trump's accomplishments include improvements in the overall economy during his term, addressing the opioid crisis that killed many Americans, working to reach agreement with the Taliban to allow the US to reduce troops in Afghanistan, approval of reduced prices for generic drugs, redesign of the North American Free Trade Agreement, Criminal Justice Reform (First Step Act), a reduction in tensions with

North Korea, attempts to limit intellectual property theft by China, and a ban on bump stocks that allow rapid fire for guns.

But there also are multiple failures in Trump's approach due to replacing policies based on human equality with those based on an ideology that puts the needs of some above those of others. These include failure to follow through on campaign promises of adding manufacturing and coal jobs, a huge tax cut that primarily benefits the most wealthy while increasing inequality, attempts to cut health insurance for millions by eliminating the Affordable Care Act, plans to reduce Social Security, Medicare and Medicaid, separating families who seek asylum at the southern border, weakening the Endangered Species Act, a reversal of carbon emission rules that will add nearly a billion tons of carbon dioxide to the atmosphere,[225] allowing greater discrimination in the workplace to accommodate employer's religious preferences,[226] repealing clean water protections, withdrawing from the long-negotiated Iran nuclear deal, pulling out of the Paris climate accord, removing forces from Syria that allowed an attack on the US allies – the Kurds – by Turkey, praising those who have transformed their democracies into dictatorships such as Putin, Duarte and Erdogan, interfering in the Mueller investigation into Russian election interference,[227] and – despite a promise to "drain the swamp" – hiring billionaires in cabinet positions whose goal is to defeat the mission of their agency (such as the Environmental Protection Agency).

His history includes bragging about inappropriate touching of women, calling Mexicans criminals and racists, running a false charity to contribute to his personal coffers that was shut down, creating a façade of a university that also was shut down, inviting officials of foreign governments to stay at his hotels, and putting up military personnel at his properties.

From the outset – beginning with his campaign – Trump has made it clear that he only intends to be president for the portion of the American people who agree with him despite claims to the contrary. His style is autocratic – not democratic. He displays a brash and combative style born of experience as a businessman who surrounded himself with people who agree with him or pretend to agree. He seeks to silence those who criticize him and intimidate those who point out his shortcomings by excoriation and lawsuits – including the press. He exhorts his followers to attack protestors at his rallies.

His false claims include stating he had the largest inaugural crowd in history, that Obama is a Muslim born in Kenya, that Russia didn't interfere in the 2016 US election (Russia's interference was agreed upon by a series of congressional investigations that included Republicans and Democrats, as well as the Mueller Report), that climate change is a hoax, and that the coronavirus also is a hoax that will be gone by April 2020 (it continues to rage).[228]

The most glaring failure of this president's character and leadership is an unwillingness to consider the equality and humanity of those he has been elected to lead. In the midst of tens of thousands of deaths from the coronavirus pandemic he is remarkably lacking in empathy and focused mainly on the "great job" he is doing. He refuses to learn from his advisors which would allow him to improve has grasp on truth and thus his performance.[229] When challenged by advisors who try to get him to change course and consider the long-term consequences of his actions rather than just ruling by whim, he fires them. They have departed at a record pace, well over 100 in his first three years.

You might think that Trump has been a successful businessman which shows that he is a good manager. But the sharp competitiveness that some businessmen use to advance themselves is not suited to governing in a democracy where the views and interests of everyone count. And we don't really know if his businesses are successful because he is the first president since Nixon to refuse to release his tax returns, and has filed perpetual lawsuits to keep them from being released. Many of his properties are losing money according to his own accountants, and he has syphoned from his charity to meet his expenses, having been forced to pay millions in fines.[230] He claims to be a billionaire and holds billions in properties, but if he is even more billions in debt he actually is a poor man. As his businesses and those of his family have lost money, the only bank that continually provides loans to cover these losses has been Deutsche Bank, and its reasons for backing him are unknown. Why would a bank provide loans to cover other questionable loans unless it was subsidized by an entity with even greater resources than the bank itself, perhaps a foreign government?[231] These questions are being probed by investigative reporters.

Most voters are economic voters, which is understandable. Ideology always yields to financial reality when one finds oneself in an economic pit with what seems like no way out. Anyone of us in that situation would grasp at any rope thrown to us. Trump's promise to restore jobs is what swung the 2016 election his way.

But his promises and confrontational style have created an army of "true believers" who have put him on a pedestal and refuse to acknowledge that he may have shortcomings. This type of blind allegiance is what has led to autocracy in many of the nations mentioned in the previous chapter. Autocrats surround themselves with "yes" people, and "yes" people tend to flock to those who offer simple solutions rather than balanced truth.

Words – especially words of leaders with a fanatical following – have consequences. In the play "Becket" by Jean Anouilh, King Henry II of England states his annoyance with the Archbishop of Canterbury: "Will no one rid me of this meddlesome priest?" Soon afterwards Henry's henchmen surround Becket and kill him at the altar. When the words of a leader inspire violent action, that leader bears responsibility.

Despite what we hear from this president and his representatives, all truths are not equal. Some of his ever-changing truths are based on emphasizing only narrow beliefs or who to blame, not actions that benefit the entire country.[232]

Once we believe in the infallibility of a leader and no longer see that person as a human being with strengths and weaknesses, we simply absorb what we are told. Paranoia becomes dominant when questions are seen as personal attacks.[233] If the person or political party you support can do no wrong in your mind then you have become part of a cult. You have given up your ability to think independently about the democratic principle of human equality and have become a danger to democracy – and to yourself – as the demagogue you support casts off supporters, as all do, at any sign of disagreement.

Countries need an infrastructure and expertise to manage mass health emergencies and must have spokespersons who can provide the public with accurate information about what to expect. Contingency plans are essential. As the COVID-19 coronavirus spread in Asia and in Europe, many countries announced plans for serious precautionary measures to limit its effects. However, because of reduced staffing at the US Center for Disease Control and a revolving door at the US Office of Homeland Security, there was little competence at the top to guide the nation and provide accurate information. The US president contradicted his own experts about the likely spread of the disease and about the time that would be required to develop a vaccine.

No matter how advanced our medical techniques become, there always will be new public health threats. This is why we must continually be alert to confront the next challenge that nature presents with all possible resources available.

We currently confront a health and financial crisis of proportions unprecedented in the last 100 years. Leaders who pay attention to the signs of an emerging crisis prepare for it, and in democracies we enlist top experts in an effort to defeat the threat. The warning systems that were designed to identify and slow such scourges like the coronavirus were ignored – first in China, which may be expected, and then in the US where the early warning systems were first dismantled and then other warnings ignored.[234] We have gone from statements by the US President that: "The Coronavirus is very much under control in the USA (February 24, 2020)," to being forced by overwhelming evidence to admit: "We're going to go through a very tough two weeks (March 31, 2020)." We expect – and should demand – the truth from our leaders rather than an ever-changing charade masquerading as truth.

In democracies that function well, "We the People" are brought into the confidence of leaders as partners in our own welfare. This has been done in wars, epidemics and economic downturns. Leaders who support democracy insist on transparency that expresses a faith in the ability of people to take their best interests into their own hands. In well-functioning democracies we have multiple eyes and ears to provide feedback and help guide our actions.

Autocrats keep information from people in an attempt to limit their input. For their ardent followers, simple answers substitute for truth, and democracy yields to the false god of personality. To the extent that the truth is hidden we move farther from democracy as our health and liberties are imperiled. In autocracies – and democracies tending to be autocratic – there are fewer voices to guide us and truth fails to reflect the real world which can have calamitous consequences.

The success of democracy depends on a public willing to pursue truth despite the uncertainty inherent in that search. It requires an informed public willing to move past the simple solutions of politicians who want to do their thinking for them. Democracy is based on the assumption that the principles of human dignity and equality must continually be renewed. Inflexible concepts do not fit a changing world. Standing up for democracy is crucial at a time when many countries are slipping into autocracy.

Action based on the best information and minds available is what allows democracies to survive. Decisive plans always must be in place based on a clear vision. When one solution fails, we must try another, informed by what we have learned and the principle of human dignity. Leaders who focus on blame and who ignore the changing reality before them are a threat to democracy. They should be removed by democratic means before autocracy permanently takes root.

Arnold Toynbee, author of the twelve volume *A Study of History* (1934-61), was considered by many the greatest historian of the twentieth century. In a broadcast of *This I Believe,* hosted by Edward R. Murrow in the early 1950s, he stated his ultimate creed.

I believe there may be some things that some people may know for certain, but I also believe that these knowable things aren't what matters most to any human being....What matters most is not one's knowledge and skill, but one's relations with other people. These relations of ours with each other... are also the really difficult things, because it is here that the question of right and wrong comes in.... We have to make the best judgment we can about what is right, and then we have to bet on it by trying to make ourselves act on it without being sure about it. Since we can never be sure, we have to try to be charitable, and open to persuasion, as we may after all have been wrong. And at the same time we have to be resolute and energetic in what we do to be effective.

The past is prescient. That's why we must do our

best to absorb the lessons of history. We may never know the whole truth, but we must take firm and timely action based on our best truths brought by inquiry and science, not our whims or those of our leaders. And then we must be willing to continually revise our actions based on new revelations.

We can focus our minds on blame, or we can move in a positive direction without losing track of lessons from the past. We can invest our energy in setting and moving toward our goals together, rather than on who is right or wrong, as we ask each other: "What kind of leadership do we need?"

At this time – and at all times – we benefit from acknowledging the truth of our interconnectedness with others and our surroundings. This is the cornerstone of democracy and the perennial key to overcoming our crises. Seeing my interests as separate from yours ensures, in the words of Benjamin Franklin, that "we will hang separately." But our salvation lies in hanging together, acknowledging our connectedness, focused on the democratic vision of human equality, with reliance on new truths as they become revealed. Some might even say that this borders on spirituality, but that's a topic for another time.

Steve Zolno is the author of two previous books: *The Future of Democracy* (2016) and *The Death of Democracy* (2018). He has been leading seminars in democracy since 2006. He is a retired healthcare manager in the San Francisco Bay Area. His website can be found at *thefutureofdemocray.net*.

Notes

1   Socrates, who had a large following, was executed in 399 BCE for teaching the youth to question authority.

2   See "Under Modi Freedom of the Press is not so free anymore."

3   "Believe in truth. To abandon facts is to abandon freedom. If nothing is true, then no one can criticize power, because there is no basis upon which to do so. If nothing is true, then all is spectacle." *On Tyranny*, Page 65.

4   First words of the Preamble to the US Constitution.

5   Lincoln's Gettysburg Address, 1863.

6   "People tend to seek out and attend to information that already confirms their beliefs." *Biased*, Page 33.

7   *The Origin of Democracy in Tribes*, Page VI, describes the "campfire democracy" of the African Bushmen, Pygmies and other band societies.

8   "Elite families lived in splendor in villas on immense estates and delighted in throwing lavish banquets attended by musicians, dancers and singers." *The Fortunes of Africa*, Page 13.

9   See "10 oldest civilizations," *www.ancienthistorylists.com/ ancient-civilizations/10-oldest-ancient-civilizations-ever-existed*

10   *A History of China*, Page 95.

11   "In 1616, a pope and a cardinal inquisitor reprimanded Galileo, warning him to curtail his forays into the supernal realms. The motions of the heavenly bodies, they said, having been touched upon in the Psalms, the Book of Joshua, and elsewhere in the Bible, were matters best left to the Holy Fathers of the Church." *Galileo's Daughter*, Page 7.

12   *Democracy*, John Dunn, Page 32.

13 From "The Funeral Oration of Pericles." *The Landmark Thucydides*, Page 112.

14 *The Cultural Origins of Human Cognition,* Pages 3-14.

15 Jean Piaget discussed how young children divide people and objects into groups in *The Construction of Reality in Child*, Page 117.

16 "If meaning is based on experience with the world – the specific actions and precepts a person has had – then it may vary from individual to individual and from culture to culture." *Louder Than Words*, Page 16.

17 "We learn what's important – the faces we see every day – and over time our brain builds a preference for those faces, at the expense of skills needed to recognize others less relevant." *Biased*, Page 14.

18 Abhijit Banerjee and Ester Duflo, who won the 2020 Nobel Prize in economics, succinctly describe the tribalism that divides us. "Over time, the instinctive defensive reaction we started from is replaced by a carefully constructed set of seemingly robust arguments. At that point, we start feeling that any disagreement with our views, given how solid the 'arguments' are, has to be either an insinuation of moral failure on our part or questioning our intelligence." *Good Economics for Hard Times*, Page 120.

19 Daniel Kahneman, in his perennial best seller, *Thinking Fast and Slow*, discusses what he considers the two major thinking systems. "System 1 operates automatically and quickly, with little or no effort and no sense of voluntary control….System 2 allocates attention to the effortful mental activities that demand it, including complex computations." Pages 20-21.

20 "A principle of organization without which a more advanced social life cannot develop in higher vertebrates is the so-called ranking order. Under this rule every individual in society knows which one is stronger and which weaker than itself." *On Aggression,* Page 44.

21 *The Origins of Political Order*, Pages 70-71.

22 See note 20, above.

23 *Democracy*. Page 26.

24 See "Fighting Breaks out in Ukraine's Parliament, Again."

25 In "all very numerous assemblies, passion never fails to wrest the scepter from reason." James Madison, in *The Federalist*, Number 55.

26 "The evidence seems to suggest even large bouts of in-migration have very little negative impact on the wages or employment prospects of the population the immigrants join." *Good Economics for Hard Times*, Page 19.

27 "Suffering comes from three quarters: from our own body... from the outer world...and finally from our relationships with other men." *Civilization and Its Discontents*, Page 28.

28 "Four score and seven years ago our fathers brought forth on this continent, a new nation, conceived in Liberty, and dedicated to the proposition that all men are created equal." *Gettysburg Address*.

29 In the 1857 *Dred Scot* case, Chief Justice Taney said that "blacks, even if free, could never be citizens because at the Founding they 'had no rights which the white man was bound to respect.' " *America's Constitution, a Biography*, Page 264.

30 In *Plessy vs. Ferguson*, 1896, the US Supreme Court upheld segregation, stating that facilities could be "separate but equal."

31 The 19th Amendment. See America's *Constitution, a Biography*, Page 403.

32 See "Labor Law Highlights, 1915-2015," by Graham Boone, Monthly Labor Review of the Bureau of Labor Statistics, October, 2015.

33 See "After the Purge, How a massive voter purge in Georgia affected the 2018 election," American Public Media Reports, October 29, 2019, by Angela Caputo, Geoff Hing, and Johnny Kauffman.

34 "Trump tells Dem congresswomen: Go back where you came from." Bianca Quilantan and David Cohen, Politico, July 14, 2019.

35 "Almost every animal capable of self-defense, from the smallest rodent upward, fights furiously when it is cornered and has no means of escape." *On Aggression*, Page 24.

36 "The desire for recognition ensures that politics will never be reducible to simple economic self-interest. Human beings make constant judgments about the intrinsic value, worth,

or dignity of other people or institutions, and they organize themselves into hierarchies based on those valuations." *The Origins of Political Order*, Page 45.

37 "Nations are doing very little to solve the most pressing issues of our time; they continue to feed the anger and distrust that polarize us." *Good Economics for Hard Times*, Page 3.

38 *Founding Brothers*, Pages 20 and 170.

39 "Here's a video of the fight that broke out on the *Texas* House floor after a Republican lawmaker said he called immigration authorities on people protesting 'sanctuary cities' legislation."

<*https://www.texastribune.org* › *2017/05/29* › *watch-fight-erupted-texas-house*>

40 See "How Finland starts its fight against fake news in primary schools." Jon Henley, 29 Jan 2020. The Guardian.

41 "...it was of great political interest to know how long it takes an average person to overcome his innate repugnance toward crime, and what exactly happens to him..." *Eichmann in Jerusalem, a Report on the Banality of Evil*, Page 92.

42 See "The failure of Democracy in Africa," by John L. Hirsch, April 15, 2011. ipinst.org.

43 "Under the 1986 provision, a person convicted of selling 5 grams of crack cocaine was required to serve a minimum sentence of five years in prison. To receive the same sentence for trafficking powder cocaine, an individual needed to possess 500 grams of cocaine – 100 time the crack cocaine amount....Overwhelmingly, those incarcerated under the federal anti-crack laws were black: for example in 1992, the figure was 91 percent and in 2006 it was 82 percent." *High Price*, Page 192.

44 This phrase is attributed to a talk by John Winthrop, a Puritan leader, in 1630, and is based on Jesus' Sermon on the Mount. It has been repeated in slightly altered form by many American politicians, including John Kennedy, Ronald Reagan and Barack Obama.

45 *The Origins of Political Order*, Page 72.

46 *SPQR: A History of Ancient Rome*, Page 478.

47 *A History of China*, Page 143.

48 *Europe*, Page 303.

49 *The Future of Democracy*, Page 56.

50 "On Educating Children." Michel de Montaigne. *The Complete Essays*, Page 163.

51 *Europe*, Pages 602-03.

52 "A progressive society counts individual variations as precious since it finds in them the means of its own growth. A democratic society must allow for intellectual freedom and the play of diverse gifts and interests in its educational measures." *Democracy and Education*, Page 217.

53 See "The Educational Theory of Robert Maynard Hutchins."

54 "How Finland starts its fight against fake news in primary schools." Jon Henly, The Guardian. January 29, 2020.

55 *The Wealth of Nations*, Book IV, Chapter II.

56 *The Wealth of Nations*, Book V, Chapter I.

57 *The Theory of Moral Sentiments*, Book I, Chapter I.

58 [Before the advent of the state] "...virtually all...peoples on earth...owed primary obligation not to a state but to kinfolk..." *The Origins of Political Order*, Page 15.

59 *Democracy*, Pages 32-33.

60 See *Constitutions of the World*.

61 "The average income of working-class Americans: $18,500...the 122 million adults in the lower half of the income pyramid." *The Triumph of Injustice*, Page 4.

62 *The Future of Democracy*, Page 28.

63 "For the thirty-odd years that separated the end of the Second World War from the OPEC Crisis, economic growth in Western Europe, the United States, and Canada was faster than it had ever been in history." *Good Economics for Hard Times*, Page 147.

64 "The need to be "business friendly" to preserve growth may be interpreted, as it was in the US and UK in the Reagan-Thatcher era, as open season for all kinds of anti-poor, pro-rich policies (such as bailouts for over-indebted corporations and wealthy individuals) that enrich the top earners at the cost of everyone else, and do nothing for growth." *Good Economics for Hard Times*, Page 204.

65 "Sky-high incomes are, for the most part, earned at the expense of the rest of society." *The Triumph of Injustice*, Page 37.

66 "After the stimulus and loose money wear off it is unlikely that growth can be sustained....Median incomes will remain flat or decline, and most families will remain economically insecure." *Aftershock*, Page 27.

67 "The Great Depression was a crisis for not just the US but for the world. It was the most serious global crisis in memory. One might think that a crisis of this magnitude would have shocked governments and central banks into action. But officials hesitated to resort to the kind of exceptional measures to which they had turned in wartime....There was a belief in the analogy between the household budget and government budget. Governments should live within their means." *Hall of Mirrors*, Page 252.

68 "Tax cuts benefitting the top 10 percent produce no significant growth in employment and income, whereas tax cuts for the bottom 90 percent do." *Good Economics for Hard Times*, Page 175.

69 *Gettysburg Address*, 1864.

70 Richard Thaler, who won the 2017 Nobel Prize in Economics, tells us that "...at any point in time an individual consists of two selves. There is a forward looking 'planner' who has good intentions and cares about the future, and a devil-may-care 'doer' who lives for the present." *Misbehaving*, Page 104.

71 *The Fortunes of Africa*, Pages 5-7.

72 "All his observations lent credence to the unpopular Sun-centered universe of Nicolaus Copernicus, which had been introduced over a half century previously, but foundered on lack of evidence. Galileo's efforts provided the beginning of a proof. And his flamboyant style of promulgating his ideas – sometimes in bawdy humorous writings, sometimes loudly at dinner parties and staged debates – transported the new astronomy from the Latin Quarters of the universities into the public arena. In 1616, a pope and a cardinal inquisitor reprimanded Galileo, warning him to curtail his forays into the supernal realms." *Galileo's Daughter*, Page 7.

73 *Einstein's Cosmos*, Page 62.

74 *Physics and Philosophy*, Page 17.

75 *The Fabric of the Cosmos,* Pages 345-47.

76 *A Universe from Nothing,* Page 69.

77 *Great Inventors and Their Inventions,* Page 192.

78 *Physics and Philosophy,* Page 66.

79 "In the sweat of your face you shall eat bread till you return to the ground, for out of it you were taken; you are dust, and to dust you shall return." Genesis 3:19, *The New Oxford Annotated Bible.*

80 See "75% of Americans now believe humans fuel climate change."

81 *The Story of Earth,* Page 258.

82 "It turned out that ...in most cases, loneliness preceded depressive symptoms...You and I exist for one reason – because those humans figured out how to cooperate. They shared their food. They looked after the sick. They were able to take down large beasts only because they were working together." *Lost Connections,* Page 93.

83 *The Green Collar Economy: How One Solution Can Fix our Two Biggest Problems. 2008.* Van Jones. Page 31.

84 See "Adapting to Rising Seas, Schools Move to the Rafters and Cats Swim."

85 See "Lead in America's water systems is a national problem."

86 See "Weedkiller products more toxic than their active ingredient, tests show."

87 See "The 'forever chemicals' fueling a public health crisis in drinking water."

88 The most accepted theory is that "they overshot the carrying capacity of their environment." *1491,* Page 281.

89 "Mayan Scientific Achievements." History.com Editors. June 7, 2019.

90 See "New study debunks myth of Cahokia's Native American lost civilization."

91 *Collapse,* Pages 574-75.

92 See "Accelerating the Low Carbon Transition: The case for stronger, more targeted and coordinated international action," Pages 12 and 58.

93 See "What is the Paris Agreement? | UNFCCC"

94 See "Trump is rolling back over 80 environmental regulations. Here are five big changes you might have missed in 2019."

95 See "Are We Really Running Out of Time to Stop Climate Change?"

96 See "America spends over $20bn per year on fossil fuel subsidies. Abolish them."

97 See "The top five states receiving subsidies are Texas, Nebraska, Kansas, Arkansas, and Illinois. Inn 2017, they received 38.5% of the $7.2 billion distributed, per the EWG Farm Subsidy Database."

98 "Renewables will have the fastest growth in the electricity sector, providing almost 30% of power demand in 2023, up from 24% in 2017." Report of the International Energy Agency, 2018.

99 See "Accelerating the Low Carbon Transition: The case for stronger, more targeted and coordinated international action." Page 96.

100 *Plan B 4.0: Mobilizing to Save Civilization.* Lester R. Brown. 2009. Pages 96-103.

101 See "Earth's Freshwater Future: Extremes of Flood and Drought."

102 See "The Amazing Water Management of the Ancient Mayans."

103 See "The Animal Origins of Coronavirus and Flu."

104 See "What is Ebola Virus Disease?" Center for Disease Control and Prevention.

105 "Report: Katrina response a 'failure of leadership,' " February 14, 2006, CNN. "The report is the result of a Republican 11-member House select committee that investigated the response to Katrina at the local, state and federal levels."

106 See "The Government had a model for handling Ebola. Trump ditched it."

107 See "Why Did the Coronavirus Outbreak Start in China?"

108 See: "Sen. Kennedy Grills DHS Chief Chad Wolf on Virus Mortality Rates."

109 See "Trade Advisor Warned White House in January of Risks of a Pandemic."

110 See "Coronavirus Risk in the U.S. 'Is Very Low,' Trump Says."

111 **The Birth of Europe**, Page 159.

112 See "How Nigeria prepared for coronavirus and why it might just avoid a major outbreak."

113 See "Share of Americans With Health Insurance Declined in 2018."

114 See "Accelerating the Low Carbon Transition," Pages 30- 39.

115 See "Giant Strides in World Health, but It Could Be So Much Better."

116 See "Americans are Retiring Later, Dying Sooner and Sicker In-Between."

117 See "The Startling Link Between Sugar and Alzheimer's."

118 See "You want a description of hell? OxyContin's 12-hour problem."

119 See "Why Living in a Poor Neighborhood Can Change Your Biology."

120 *Lost Connections*, Page 86.

121 *Lost Connections*, Page 93.

122 *Lost Connections*, Page 100.

123 *Never Enough*, Page 6.

124 *Never Enough*, Page 3.

125 See "*Social Relationships and Health: A Flashpoint for Health Policy.*"

126 See "A Bridge to Brainpower?"

127 See "What Was George W. Bush's Greatest Achievement?"

128 *The Varieties of Religious Experience*, Page 15.

129 *The Origins and History of Consciousness*, Page 6.

130 *SPQR*, Pages 73 and 275.

131 *Walking the Bible*, Page 174.

132 *Philosophies of India*, Page 52.

133 *Philosophies of India*, Page 381.

134 *China*, Pages 69-70.

135 "A principle of organization without which a more advanced social life cannot develop in higher vertebrates is the so-called ranking order. Under this rule every individual in society knows which one is stronger and which weaker than itself." *On Aggression*, Page 44.

136 Exodus 18:13-26

137 Exodus 20:1-17

138 *Two Treatises of Government*, First Treatise, Chap IV, Section 24.

139 *Common Sense and The American Crisis I*, Page 4.

140 Cass Sunstein states: "New norms, and laws that entrench or fortify them, can give rise to beliefs, preferences, and values that did not exist before." *How Change Happens*, Page 4.

141 *Marbury vs. Madison*, 1803. Quoted in *The Jurisprudence of John Marshall*, Page 204.

142 *McCullough vs. Maryland*, 1819. Quoted in *The Jurisprudence of John Marshall*, Page 82.

143 *The Future of Democracy*, Pages 168 and 180.

144 *A Theory of Justice*, Page 53.

145 George Washington's Farewell Address.

146 *Natural Law and Natural Rights*, Pages 161-163.

147 "[Europeans] paid little attention to the news, at the end of June, that Archduke Franz Ferdinand of Austria-Hungary and his wife, Sophie, had been killed by an assassin's bullet in the provincial city of Sarajevo." *To End All Wars*, Page 76.

148 *To End All Wars*, Pages 355-58.

149 *The Politics of International Economic Relationships*, Page 14.

150 *Good Economics for Hard Times*, Page 147.

151 *The Politics of International Economic Relationships*, Page 16.

152 Example: Richard Nixon. "His tacit support for the coup in Chile that replaced democratically elected president Salvador Allende with the repressive regime of Augusto Pinochet in 1973…" *Do Morals Matter?* Page 90.

153 See "Hong Kong on Strike: The picket line could be a powerful tool in the fight for democracy."

154 See "Margaret Thatcher, 'Iron Lady' Who Set Britain on a New Course, Dies at 87."

155 "Ronald Reagan would return time and again to the image of the so-called "welfare queen," who was black, lazy, female and fraudulent. The model for this was Linda Taylor, a woman from Chicago who had four aliases and was convicted of $8,000 in fraud, for which she spent several years in prison…one and one half more years than Charles Keating, the central figure in the most corrupt scandal of the Reagan era, and the related Savings and Loan crisis that was to cost taxpayers over $500 billion in bailout money. [Taylor was sentenced to 2-6 years and spent two years in prison. Keating spent 4 ½ years] Reagan: 'We're in danger of creating a permanent culture of poverty…misguided welfare programs instituted in the name of compassion have actually helped turn a shrinking problem into a national tragedy.' " *Good Economics for Hard Times*, Page 284.

156 Including a 1983 invasion of Grenada and a 1996 attack on Libya. *Tear Down This Myth*, Page 89.

157 *Israel/Palestine*, Page 130.

158 *Do Morals Matter?* Page 139.

159 *Black Wave*, Page 28.

160 "The president who is today hailed as a modern savior of the American economy saw poverty actually increase while he was in the White House….There was something else that took off during the Reagan years: a sense that greed was taking over America." *Tear Down this Myth*, Page 67.

161 "Five years into the rule of Erdogan, Putin, and Chavez, many outside observers believe that they were strengthening democratic institutions in their countries….It wasn't until these strongmen gained a second or even a third victory at the polls that they completed their countries' descent toward outright dictatorship." *The People vs. Democracy*, Page 188.

162 "The main trend of the Venezuela experience of dismantling democracy from within is that the process aimed to replace representative democracy with 'participatory democracy,' used democratic tools but defrauded democracy itself." *Dismantling Democracy in Venezuela*, Page 33.

163 *The Man Without a Face*, Page 151.

164 See "Europe must stop this disgrace: Viktor Oban is dismantling democracy."

165 *The People vs. Democracy*, Page 10.

166 See "The average family can't afford to buy a home in 71 percent of the country."

167 "Although immigrants consume public services, they also pay taxes, on balance contributing more than they take." *The Populist Temptation*, Page 156.

168 *The People vs. Democracy*, Page 108.

169 See "49% of Americans Expect To Live Paycheck To Paycheck This Year."

170 "Seeing political institutions as captured and irredeemably corrupt, they [populist leaders] will seek to advance the interests of their followers by weakening the system. Even when they take office through legitimate means...they may advance legislation or issue emergency decrees that that abrogate the operation of representative institutions...They may use force or violence, or at least fail to curtail them, while curtailing the rights of minorities and denying the legitimacy of rival politicians and governments." *The Populist Temptation*, Page 9.

171 "Wages and employment...suddenly exposed to Chinese competition remained depressed for more than a decade....Prior to the 1970s, when growth was rapid, it was still possible to argue that foreign trade raised all boats." *The Populist Temptation*, Page 109.

172 "This is how democracies now die. Blatant dictatorship — in the form of fascism, communism, or military rule — has disappeared across much of the world. Military coups and other violent seizures of power are rare. Most countries hold regular elections. Since the end of the Cold War, most democratic breakdowns have been caused not by generals and soldiers but by elected governments themselves. Like Chávez in Venezuela, elected leaders have subverted democratic institutions in Georgia, Hungary, Nicaragua, Peru, the Philippines, Poland, Russia, Sri Lanka, Turkey, and Ukraine. Democratic backsliding today begins at the ballot box." *How Democracies Die*, Page 5.

173 *Do Morals Matter?* Page 163.

174 See "Trump set a dangerous precedent abandoning American allies" Lauren Frias. Nov 14, 2019. Business Insider.

175 *Europe*, Page 657.

176 See "The Third of May, 1791."

177 "This impulse is reinforced, in Poland as well as in Hungary and many other formerly Communist countries, by the widespread feeling that the rules of competition are flawed because the reforms of the 1990s were unfair." From "A Warning from Europe: The Worst Is Yet To Come."

178 See "1946 US report said 'Poles persecuted the Jews as vigorously as did the Germans."

179 See "The Truth about Poland's Role in the Holocaust."

180 "In 2015, the [European] Commission launched an investigation...of Polish legislation...that compromised the independence of the...country's Supreme Court, and that subjected Poland's public broadcasters to state control." *The Populist Temptation*, Page 143.

181 "From a democratic standpoint it is not enough to have nonoppressive institutions that enforce rules. Accountability, participation, and persuasion are also essential." *Power and Governance in a Partially Globalized World*, Page 261.

182 *Leviathan*, Chapter XIII, Paragraph 9.

183 See the *Funeral Oration of Pericles*, footnote #13.

184 *The Future of Democracy*, Page 160.

185 "Inequality has risen dramatically in recent years, with searing consequences for societies across the world." *Good Economics for Hard Times*, Page 226.

186 "63 percent of those is a survey said they are not engaged – finding no meaning – in their work." *Lost Connections*, Page 77.

187 See "What did China know about coronavirus, and when?"

188 See "Coronavirus strikes UK Prime Minister Boris Johnson, his health secretary and his chief medical adviser."

189 See "How South Korea Solved Its Acute Hospital-Bed Shortage."

190 See "What The US Could Learn From Nigeria's Response To The COVID-19 Coronavirus Outbreak."

191   See "The missing six weeks: how Trump failed the biggest test of his life."

192 See "Coronavirus response so far sidelines CDC." March 25, 2020. USA TODAY.

193   See "Job Vacancies and Inexperience Mar Federal Response to Coronavirus."

194 *Hamilton, Adams, Jefferson*, Pages 132-34.

195 *The Future of Democracy*, Pages 188-89.

196 *The Oxford History of the American People*, Pages 411-14.

197 *The Oxford History of the American People*, Page 410.

198   "Lincoln's political genius...enabled him to form friendships with men who had previously opposed him; to repair injured feelings that, left unattended, might have escalated into permanent hostility; to assume responsibility for the failures of subordinates; to share credit with ease; and to learn from mistakes." *Team of Rivals*, Page xvii.

199 Lincoln's Second Inaugural Address, 1865.

200 *Team of Rivals*, Pages 354-55.

201 *An Indigenous People's History of the United States*, Page 305.

202 *The Oxford History of the American People*, Page 852.

203 See "Woodrow Wilson was extremely racist — even by the standards of his time." Dylan Matthews. Nov 20, 2015. VOX.

204 *The Oxford History of the American People*, Pages 941-46.

205 *Three Days at the Brink*, Page 132.

206 *Three Days at the Brink*, Page 140.

207 *Truman*, Page 449.

208 *The Oxford History of the American People*, Pages 1079-80.

209 *Do Morals Matter?* Page 64.

210 *Justice for All*, Page 324.

211 *Do Morals Matter?* Page 73.

212 *The Years of Lyndon Johnson: The Passage of Power.* Page 538.

213 *Do Morals Matter?* Page 85.

214 See "Landmark Laws of the Lyndon B. Johnson Administration."

215 *Do Morals Matter?* Page 104.

216 *Do Morals Matter?* Pages 120-23.

217 *Day of Reckoning: The Consequences of American Economic Policy*, Page 91.

218 *Do Morals Matter?* Page 134.

219 *Israel/Palestine*, Page 158.

220 "[A] study shows that tax cuts benefitting the top 10 percent produce no significant growth in employment and income, whereas tax cuts for the bottom 90 percent do." *Good Economics For Hard Times.* Page 175.

221 *Do Morals Matter?* Page 146.

222 *Angler: The Cheney Vice Presidency*, Page 132.

223 *Do Morals Matter?* Page 157.

224 See "Pity the sad legacy of Barack Obama," or "Barack Obama's original sin: America's post-racial illusion."

225 See "Trump to Deal Final Blow to Car Pollution Goals."

226 See "Despite the Coronavirus Pandemic, the Government Is Still Targeting L.G.B.T.Q Rights."

227 "The President engaged in...public attacks on the investigation, non-public efforts to control it, and efforts both public and private to encourage witnesses not to cooperate with the investigation." *Mueller Report*, Page 7.

228 See "From 'hoax' to pandemic: Trump's shifting rhetoric on coronavirus."

229 *Do Morals Matter?* Page 177.

230 See "Trump Ordered to Pay $2 Million to Charities for Misuse of Foundation."

231 *Dark Towers*, Pages 310-18.

232 "Post-truth amounts to a form of ideological supremacy, whereby its practitioners are trying to compel someone to believe in something whether there is good evidence for it or not. And this is the recipe for political domination." *Post-Truth*, Page 13.

233   See "I wrote 'The Art of the Deal' with Trump. His self-sabotage is rooted in his past."

234 See "Trump Shrugged Off Repeated Intelligence Warnings About Coronavirus Pandemic."

References

"Accelerating the Low Carbon Transition: The case for stronger, more targeted and coordinated international action." David G. Victor, Frank W. Geels, Simon Sharpe. Commissioned by the UK Government Department for Business, Energy and Industrial Strategy. November, 2019.

"Adapting to Rising Seas, Schools Move to the Rafters and Cats Swim." Hannah Beech and Jes Aznar. February 22, 2020. New York Times.

"After the Purge, How a massive voter purge in Georgia affected the 2018 election." American Public Media Reports, by Angela Caputo, Geoff Hing, and Johnny Kauffman. October 29, 2019.

Aftershock. Robert Reich. 2011, 2013. Vintage.

"The Amazing Water Management of the Ancient Mayans." May 18, 2018. Scribol.

"America spends over $20bn per year on fossil fuel subsides. Abolish them." Dan Nuccitelli. July 30, 2018. The Guardian.

"Americans Are Retiring Later, Dying Sooner and Sicker In-Between." Ben Silverman. October 23, 2017. Bloomberg.

Angler: The Cheney Vice Presidency. Barton Gellman. 2008. Penguin Press.

"The Animal Origins of Coronavirus and Flu." Tara C. Smith. February 25, 2020. Quanta Magazine.

"Are We Really Running Out of Time to Stop Climate Change?" Rafi Letzter, Live Science, September 26, 2019.

"The average family can't afford to buy a home in 71 percent of the country." December 17, 2019. CBS Moneywatch.

America's Constitution, a Biography. Akhil Reed Amar. 2005. Random House.

"Barack Obama's original sin: America's post-racial illusion." Keeanga-Yamahtta Taylor. January 13, 2017. The Atlantic.

Biased. Jennifer Eberhardt. 2019. Viking.

Black Wave. Saudi Arabia, Iran, and the Forty Year Rivalry that Unraveled Culture, Religion, and Collective Memory in the Middle East. Kim Ghattas. 2020. Henry Holt.

The Birth of Europe. Jacque Le Goff. 2005, 2007. Blackwell.

"A Bridge to Brainpower? Playing your cards right can help keep you sharp long after retirement." Jon Saraceno. AARP Bulletin. Undated.

China, A History. John Keay. 2009. Basic Books.

Civilization and Its Discontents. Sigmund Freud. [1930] 2011. Martino Publishing.

Collapse: How Societies Choose to Fail or Succeed. Jared Diamond. 2005. Viking.

Common Sense and The American Crisis I. Thomas Paine. [1776] 2012, 2015. Penguin.

The Complete Essays. Michel de Montaigne. 1987, 1991, 2000. Penguin.

Constitutions of the World. Robert L. Maddex. 1996, 2014. Routledge.

The Construction of Reality in the Child. Jean Piaget. 1954. Basic Books.

"Coronavirus Risk in the U.S. 'Is Very Low,' Trump Says." Michael D. Shear and Katie Rogers. Feb. 26, 2020. New York Times.

"Coronavirus strikes UK Prime Minister Boris Johnson, his health secretary and his chief medical adviser." Angela Dewan and Sarah Dean. March 27, 2020. CNN.

The Cultural Origins of Human Cognition. Michael Tomasello. 1999. Harvard University Press.

Dark Towers: Deutsche Bank, Donald Trump, and an Epic Trail of Destruction. David Enrich. 2020. Harper Collins.

Day of Reckoning: The Consequences of American Economic Policy. Benjamin Friedman. 1988, 1989. Vintage Books.

Democracy. John Dunn. 2005. Atlantic Monthly Press.

Democracy and Education. John Dewey. [1916] 2013. Published by Create Space.

"Despite the Coronavirus Pandemic, the Government Is Still Targeting L.G.B.T.Q. Rights." Jeffery Toobin. April 20, 2020. New Yorker.

Dismantling Democracy in Venezuela: The Chavez Authoritarian Experience. Allan Brewer Carías. 2010. Cambridge University Press.

Do Morals Matter? Presidents and Foreign Policy from FDR to Trump. Joseph Nye. 2020. Oxford.

Earth's Freshwater Future: Extremes of Flood and Drought. Ellen Gray. June 13, 2019. NASA.

"The Educational Theory of Robert M. Hutchins." 2000. New Foundations.

Eichmann in Jerusalem, a Report on the Banality of Evil. 1963. Hannah Arendt. Viking.

Einstein's Cosmos. Michio Kaku. 2004. W.W. Norton.

Europe. Norman Davies. 1996, 1998. Harper Perennial.

"Europe must stop this disgrace: Viktor Orban is dismantling democracy." Timothy Garton Ash. June 20, 2019. The Guardian.

The Fabric of the Cosmos. Brian Greene. 2004, 2005. Vintage.

"Fighting Breaks out in Ukraine's Parliament, Again. The brawl started over a poster labeling a politician 'Putin's agent.'" This was the latest of several fights between Ukrainian lawmakers in recent years. December 20, 2018. NBC News.

"The 'forever chemicals' fueling a public health crisis in drinking water." Tom Perkins. February 3, 2020. The Guardian.

"49% of Americans Expect To Live Paycheck To Paycheck This Year." Zack Friedman. February 19, 2020. Forbes.

The Fortunes of Africa. Martin Meredith. 2014. Simon and Schuster.

1491. Charles C. Mann. 2011. Vintage

"From 'hoax' to pandemic: Trump's shifting rhetoric on coronavirus." Sam Ball. 3/20/2020. France 24.

The Future of Democracy. Steve Zolno. 2016-2018. Regent Press.

Founding Brothers. Joseph J. Ellis. 2000. Knopf.

Galileo's Daughter. Dava Sobel. 1999. Walkers Publishers.

"Giant Strides in World Health, but It Could Be So Much Better." Austin Frakt and Aaron E. Carroll, Feb. 4, 2019, NY Times.

Good Economics for Hard Times. Abhijit Banerjee and Ester Duflo. 2019. Public Affairs.

"The government had a model for handling Ebola. Trump ditched it." John Harwood. February 26, 2020. CNN.

Great Inventor and Their Inventions. Frank B. Bachman. 1918. American Book Company.

The Green Collar Economy: How One Solution Can Fix Our Two Biggest Problems. Van Jones. 2008. HarperCollins.

Hall of Mirrors: The Great Depression, the Great Recession, and the Uses – and Misuses – of History. Barry Eichengreen, 2016. Oxford.

Hamilton, Adams, Jefferson. Darren Staloff. 2005. Hill and Wang.

"Hong Kong on Strike: The picket line could be a powerful tool in the fight for democracy." Dominic Chiu, Tiffany Wong. July 3, 2019. Foreign Policy

Magazine.

How Change Happens. Cass Sunstein. 2019. MIT Press.

How Democracies Die. Steven Livitsky and Daniel Ziblatt. 2018. Crown.

"How South Korea Solved Its Acute Hospital-Bed Shortage." Dasl Yoon. March 22, 2020. Wall Street Journal.

"How Nigeria prepared for coronavirus and why it might just avoid a major outbreak." Chikwe Ihekweazu, CEO of the Nigerian Center for Disease Control. February 28, 2020. Quartz.

"How Finland starts its fight against fake news in primary schools." Jon Henly. January 29, 2020. The Guardian.

The Idea of Justice. Amartya Sen. 2009. Harvard University Press.

An Indigenous Peoples' History of the United States. Roxanne Dunbar-Ortiz. 2014. Beacon Press.

Israel/Palestine. Alan Dowty. 2017. Polity.

"I wrote 'The Art of the Deal' with Trump. His self-sabotage is rooted in his past." Tony Schwartz. May 16, 2017. Washington Post.

"Job Vacancies and Inexperience Mar Federal Response to Coronavirus." Jennifer Steinhauser and Zolan Kanno-Youngs. March 26, 2020. New York Times.

The Jurisprudence of John Marshall. Robert Kenneth Faulkner. 1968. Princeton University Press.

Justice for All: Earl Warren and the Nation He Made. Jim Newton. 2007. Penguin.

"Landmark Laws of the Lyndon B. Johnson Administration." on the LBJ Library Website.

The Landmark Thucydides. Edited by Robert B. Strassler. 1996, Free Press.

Leviathan. Thomas Hobbes. [1651] 1996, 1998, Oxford University Press.

"The Law Collection of Ur-Nammi." Miguel Civil, in *Cuneiform Royal Inscriptions and Related Texts in the Schøyen Collection*, 221–286. Edited by A.R. George. 2011. Cornell University Press.

"Lead in America's water systems in a national problem." Rachel Layne. November 18, 2018. Moneywatch.

Lost Connections: Why You're Depressed and How to Find Hope. Johann Hari. 2018. Bloomsbury Publishing.

Louder Than Words. Ben Bergen. 2012. Basic Books.

The Man Without a Face. Masha Gessen. 2012. Riverhead Books.

"Margaret Thatcher, 'Iron Lady' Who Set Britain on a New Course, Dies at 87." Joseph R. Gregory. April 8, 2013. New York Times.

"Mayan Scientific Achievements." June 7, 2019. History.com Editors.

Misbehaving: The Making of Behavioral Economics. Richard Thaler. 2015. W. W. Norton.

"The Missing Six Weeks: how Trump failed the biggest test of his life." Ed Pilkington and Tom McCarthy. March 28, 2020. The Guardian.

Natural Law and Natural Rights. John Finnis. 1980-2002. Clarendon Law Series, Oxford.

Never Enough: The Neuroscience and Experience of Addiction. Judith Grisel. 2019. Doubleday.

The New Oxford Annotated Bible. Revised Standard Edition. 1962, 1973. Oxford University Press.

"New study debunks myth of Cahokia's Native American lost civilization." Yasmin Anwar. January 2, 2020. University of California - Berkeley.

"1946 US report said 'Poles persecuted the Jews as vigorously as did the Germans." David Sedley. March 1, 2018. Times of Israel.

On Aggression. Conrad Lorenz. 1963, 1966. Harcourt.

"On Educating Children." Michel de Montaigne. *The Complete Essays.* 1987-2003. Penguin.

On Tyranny. Timothy Snyder. 2017. Penguin Random

House.

The Origin of Democracy in Tribes. Ronald M. Glassman. 2017. Springer.

The Origins and History of Consciousness. Erich Neumann. 1954. 1973. Bollingen.

The Origins of Political Order. Francis Fukuyama. 2011, 2012. Farrar, Strauss, and Giroux.

The Oxford History of the American People. Samuel Eliot Morison. 1965. Oxford University Press.

The People vs. Democracy. Yascha Mounk. 2018. Harvard University Press.

Philosophies of India. Heinrich Zimmer. 1951, 1974. Bollingen.

Physics and Philosophy. Werner Heisenberg. [1958] 2007. Harper Perennial Edition.

"Pity the sad legacy of Barack Obama." Cornell West. January 9, 2017, The Atlantic.

Plan B 4.0. Mobilizing to Save Civilization. Lester R. Brown. 2009. W. W. Norton.

The Politics of International Economic Relations. Joan E. Spero and Jeffery A Hunt. 2003. Thomson Wadsworth.

The Populist Temptation. Barry Eichengreen. 2018. Oxford University Press.

Post-Truth. Lee McIntyre. 2018. Massachusetts Institute of Technology.

Power and Governance in a Partially Globalized World. Robert Keohane. 2002. Routledge.

Presidential Leadership in Crisis. Kenneth T. Walsh. 2020. Routledge.

"Report On The Investigation Into Russian Interference In The 2016 Presidential Election." March, 2019. Special Counsel Robert S. Mueller, III.

"Report: Katrina response a 'failure of leadership,'" February 14, 2006, CNN.

The Rise and Fall of the Roman Empire. Edward Gibbon. 1776. Fred de Fau and Company.

"75% of Americans now believe humans fuel climate change." Stephen Johnson. September 16, 2019. Think Big.

"Sen. Kennedy Grills DHS Chief Chad Wolf on Virus Mortality Rates." Neil Munro. February 26, 2020. Breitbart.

"Senator says White House turned down emergency coronavirus funding in early February." Suzanne Smalley. March 27, 2020. Yahoo News.

"Share of Americans With Health Insurance Declined in 2018." Margot Sanger-Katz. September 19, 2019. New York Times.

"Social Relationships and Health: A Flashpoint for Health Policy." Debra Umberson and Jennifer Karas Montez. Aug 4, 2011. US Department of Health and Human Services.

SPQR: A History of Ancient Rome. Mary Beard. 2015. W.W. Norton.

"The Startling Link Between Sugar and Alzheimer's. A high-carb diet, and the attendant high blood sugar, are associated with cognitive decline." Olga Khazan. Jan 26, 2018. The Atlantic.

The Story of Earth. Robert M. Hazen. 2013, 2014. Penguin.

"Syrian ceasefire has failed as civilians killed daily: UN." January 17, 2020. UN News.

Team of Rivals. Doris Kearns Goodwin. 2006. Simon and Schuster.

Tear Down This Myth. Will Bunch. 2009. Free Press.

A Theory of Justice. John Rawls. 1971, 1999. Belknap Press.

The Theory of Moral Sentiments. Adam Smith [1759] 2015. Pantianos Classics Reprint.

"The Third of May, 1791." Norman Davies. May 15, 1991. Presentation at Department of History, Harvard.

Three Days on the Brink. Bret Baier. 2019. William Morrow.

"The top five states receiving subsidies are Texas, Nebraska, Kansas, Arkansas, and Illinois. Inn 2017, they received 38.5% of the $7.2 billion distributed, per the EWG Farm Subsidy Database." Kimberly Amadeo. July 4, 2019. The Balance, U.S. Economy and News.

To End All Wars: A Story of Loyalty and Rebellion, 1914-1918. Adam Hochschild. 2011. Mariner.

Transforming Depression. David Rosen. 1993, 2002. Nicolas Hays.

The Triumph of Injustice. Emmanuel Saez and Gabriel Zucman. 2019. William Morrow.

Truman. David McCullough. 1992. Simon and Schuster.

"Trump is rolling back over 80 environmental regulations. Here are five big changes you might have missed in 2019." Emma Newburger. December 24, 2019. CNBC.

"Trump officials did sound the coronavirus alarm. They just don't work there anymore." Merdith McGraw. 3/12/20. POLITICO.

"Trump Ordered to Pay $2 Million to Charities for Misuse of Foundation." Alan Feuer, Nov. 22, 2019, New York Times.

"Trump set a dangerous precedent abandoning American allies." Lauren Frias. Nov 14, 2019. Business Insider.

"Trump Shrugged Off Repeated Intelligence Warnings About Coronavirus Pandemic." Mary Papenfuss. March 20, 2020. Huffington Post.

"Trump to Deal Final Blow to Car Pollution Goals." Coral Davenport. March 31, 2020. New York Times.

"The Truth about Poland's Role in the Holocaust." Edna Friedberg. February 6, 2018. The Atlantic.

Two Treatises of Government. John Locke. [1690] 1960-1992. Press Syndicate of the University of Cambridge.

"Under Modi Freedom of the Press is not so free

anymore." Vindu Goel and Jeffrey Gettlemen. April 3, 2020. New York Times.

A Universe from Nothing. Lawrence Krause. 2012. Free Press.

"U.S. Jobs Trail Forecasts; Wages Rise Least Since Mid-2018." Reade Picket. January 10, 2020. Bloomberg.

The Varieties of Religious Experience, A Study in Human Nature. William James. [1902] 2009. Seven Treasures Publications.

Walking the Bible. Bruce Feiler. 2001, 2014. William Morrow Publishing.

"A Warning From Europe: The Worst Is Yet To Come." Anne Applebaum. October, 2018 issue of The Atlantic.

The Wealth of Nations. Adam Smith. [1776] 2004. Barnes and Noble.

"Weedkiller products more toxic than their active ingredients, tests show." Carey Gillam. May 8, 2018.The Guardian.

"What did China know about coronavirus, and when?" James Leggate., March 20, 2020. FOX Business.

"What happened to the ancient Mayans?" Matthew Black. October 18, 2018. History 101.

"What is Ebola Virus Disease?" Center for Disease Control and Prevention.

"What is the Paris Agreement?" UNFCCC. 2015.

"What The US Could Learn From Nigeria's Response To The COVID-19 Coronavirus Outbreak." Andrew Wight., Mar 24, 2020. Forbes.

"What Was George W. Bush's Greatest Achievement?" John Seven. August 1, 2018. Inside History Newsletter.

"Why Did the Coronavirus Outbreak Start in China?" Yi-Zheng Lian. Feb. 20, 2020. New York Times.

"Why Living in a Poor Neighborhood Can Change Your Biology." Andrew Curry. June 14, 2018. Nautilus Magazine.

"Woodrow Wilson was extremely racist — even by the standards of his time." Dylan Matthews. Nov 20, 2015. VOX.

The Years of Lyndon Johnson: The Passage of Power. Robert Caro. 2012. Knopf.

"You want a description of hell? OxyContin's 12-hour problem." Harriet Ryan, Lisa Girion and Scott Glover. May 5, 2016. LA Times.